CREATIVE STATES OF MIND

What is it like to be an artist? Drawing on interviews with professional artists, this book takes the reader inside the creative process. The author, an artist and a psychotherapist, uses psychoanalytic theory to shed light on fundamental questions such as the origin of new ideas and the artist's state of mind while working.

Based on interviews with 33 professional artists, who reflect on their experiences of creating new works of art, as well as her own artistic practice, Patricia Townsend traces the trajectory of the creative process from the artist's first inkling or 'pre-sense', through to the completion of a work, and its release to the public. Drawing on psychoanalytic theory, particularly the work of Donald Winnicott, Marion Milner and Christopher Bollas, the book presents the artist's process as a series of interconnected and overlapping stages, in which there is a movement between the artist's inner world, the outer world of shared 'reality', and the spaces in-between.

Creative States of Mind: Psychoanalysis and the Artist's Process fills an important gap in the psychoanalytic theory of art by offering an account of the full trajectory of the artist's process based on the evidence of artists themselves. It will be useful to artists who want to understand more about their own processes, to psychoanalysts and psychotherapists in their clinical work, and to anyone who studies the creative process.

Patricia Townsend is an artist, working with video, photography and installation, and a psychoanalytic psychotherapist. Her artworks have been exhibited widely and her writing on psychoanalysis and the artist's process has appeared in a variety of publications. She recently completed a PhD at the Slade School of Fine Art, University College London.

'This is a highly original and extremely rich study of the artistic process as one of creative *processing*, or *working through*. Valuably based on interviews with other artists as well as on Townsend's self-reflection on her own artwork, this book compellingly argues that artistic forms grow out of our inner worlds but are not simply a representation of these. This study is the most resonant and detailed psychoanalytic account of creative processes that I have read since the work of Marion Milner. Like Milner's contributions to our understanding of art, it should be an essential read for artists as well as for those who study them, or seek to understand artworks.'

Catherine Grant, Professor of Digital Media and
Screen Studies, Birkbeck, University of London.

'Psychoanalysis has struggled to understand the process of artistic creativity *from the inside*, but Patricia Townsend's outstanding book draws on interviews with professional artists as well as her own experience to investigate the process, from the artist's first awareness of a creative work through to its emergence into the world. Taking cues from Donald Winnicott, Marion Milner and Christopher Bollas in particular she builds a convincing and subtle account of the unfolding creative act, which will engage anyone interested in how it is that we relate creatively to our worlds.'

Ken Robinson, Psychoanalyst, Visiting Professor of
Psychoanalysis, Northumbria University.

CREATIVE STATES OF MIND

Psychoanalysis and the Artist's Process

Patricia Townsend

Routledge
Taylor & Francis Group

LONDON AND NEW YORK

First published 2019
by Routledge
2 Park Square, Milton Park, Abingdon, Oxon OX14 4RN

and by Routledge
52 Vanderbilt Avenue, New York, NY 10017

Routledge is an imprint of the Taylor & Francis Group, an informa business

British Library Cataloguing-in-Publication Data
A catalogue record for this book is available from the British Library

Library of Congress Cataloging-in-Publication Data
Names: Townsend, Patricia, 1947– author.
Title: Creative states of mind/Patricia Townsend.
Other titles: The artist's creative process
Description: New York : Routledge, 2019. | Edited version of the
    author's thesis (doctoral—University College, 2018) under the
    title: The artist's creative process : a Winnicottian view. | Includes
    bibliographical references.
Identifiers: LCCN 2018046812 (print) | LCCN 2018047402 (ebook) |
    ISBN 9780429052736 (Master eBook) | ISBN 9780367146146
    (hardback) | ISBN 9780367146160 (pbk.)
Subjects: LCSH: Art—Psychology. | Creation (Literary, artistic, etc.)
Classification: LCC N71 (ebook) | LCC N71 .T69 2019 (print) | DDC
    700.1/9—dc23
LC record available at https://lccn.loc.gov/2018046812

ISBN: 978-0-367-14614-6 (hbk)
ISBN: 978-0-367-14616-0 (pbk)
ISBN: 978-0-429-05273-6 (ebk)

Typeset in Bembo
by Apex CoVantage, LLC

MIX
Paper from
responsible sources
FSC   FSC® C013056
www.fsc.org

Printed and bound in Great Britain by
TJ International Ltd, Padstow, Cornwall

CONTENTS

ILLUSTRATIONS

FOREWORD

Freud's attitude to artistic creation was complex and contradictory, for while he loved the arts and held them in high regard, he treated them as quasi-neurotic phenomena when he viewed them through his psychoanalytic lens. This pathological bias cast a shadow over psychoanalytic writing for years to come, and the idea that art is a devious expression of repressed impulses has influenced the way that art is viewed to the present day. It has led to a complicated relationship between psychoanalysis and art, for while psychoanalysis can fascinate by seeming to reveal the 'secrets' of art, it is frequently criticised for reducing it to its basic elements and thus devaluing it.

There is little doubt that this pathological, reductive skew has curtailed more open exploration of artistic creativity from a psychoanalytic perspective. Although many analysts have questioned Freud's original approach, attempts to create alternative theories have been few. It is true that the Kleinian school, in the work of Hanna Segal, has developed a more comprehensive theory of artistic creation, but as in Freud's original model, this is tied to a theoretical shibboleth, the need of the artist to make reparation for primitive destructive impulses.

Creativity and imagination have long been of interest to Independent psychoanalysts of the British Society but, although their ideas are often suggestive, no coherent theory of artistic creation has emerged from their writing. Winnicott's work is a case in point, for while it establishes a radically new conceptual space for thinking about art, its novel dimensions are never completely worked out. The closed conceptual system was contrary to Winnicott's way of thinking and, in contrast to Freud, he never tried to set out his ideas in the form of a finished theory.

Winnicott's writing on creativity exemplifies this, for while he insisted, against Melanie Klein, on the crucial role of the mother's responsiveness in infant development and explored the origins of creativity in this adaptive relationship, he never developed a theory of art in its own right. He traced a line from the infant's *primary creativity* (creating the breast that the mother provides) through *transitional phenomena* and childhood play to adult creativity, including the arts, but was more concerned with creative living as a universal potential than with its specific development in the creative arts.

For the psychoanalytic observer interested in art, this gap in theory is a tantalising challenge: can psychoanalysis throw light on art without reducing and devaluing it? The author of this book, Patricia Townsend, is both artist and psychoanalytic psychotherapist, and this unique position informs her approach. As artist, she explores the phenomenology of artistic creation, using her own experience and that of the many professional artists whom she interviewed to take us *into* the creative experience. She shows us what it is like to *be* the artist and allows us to glimpse the creative process from its first stirrings as 'hunch', or 'pre-sense', to its gradual emergence as material form. She allows us to share in the difficulties of entering a creative state of mind and the satisfactions, tempered with disillusionment, of creating a work. Out of this raw material, she extracts recurrent themes and, as psychoanalytic observer, she explores these in the light of contemporary psychoanalytic ideas. Her approach leans heavily, but not exclusively, on Donald Winnicott, Marion Milner and Christopher Bollas, but she also draws on non-analytic sources, in particular the work of Anton Ehrenzweig and Susanne Langer.

This book fills an important gap in psychoanalytic theorising about art and offers a coherent account of the artistic process from an independent perspective. I predict it will become an important source book for writers on art, and it lays the foundation for a more relational view of art and the function it has in the lives of both artist and viewer.

Ken Wright
July 2018

ACKNOWLEDGEMENTS

This book is based on research undertaken whilst I was a PhD candidate at the Slade School of Fine Art, University College London. I am very grateful to Professor Sharon Morris, Professor Lesley Caldwell and Dr Ken Wright, for their invaluable help, advice and support throughout the long process of conducting the research and writing the PhD thesis. I am also grateful to Simon Faithfull, whose creative insights always took me a few steps further in the development of my artworks. I would like to thank Professor Catherine Grant and Professor Ken Robinson for their very helpful comments on my thesis, and Professor Juliet Mitchell for her encouragement in relation to the 'Making Space' conference held at UCL in 2012 and the Special Edition of *Free Associations* I guest edited (Townsend, 2014). Special thanks go to Peter for his support throughout and for his practical help, particularly with exhibitions.

Finally, I want to express my gratitude to the artists who allowed me to interview them and who made this project possible. I am deeply grateful for their generosity in speaking so openly about their creative processes and for allowing me to quote from their interviews in this research. Their contributions are at the heart of this book.

INTRODUCTION

What happens in the mind of an artist as he or she creates a new work of art? Is it possible to understand and explain artists' states of mind or, as many believe, is the creative process so elusive and mysterious that any attempt to grasp it is doomed to failure? The seeds of this book were sown when, as a practising artist, I began to ask myself these questions, becoming increasingly curious about my own process of making art. I tried to pinpoint the moment when a new work begins and realised that, at first, I often have a vague intimation of what I want my subject to be but little sense of what form the potential new artwork might take. Sometimes there is a long time gap before an idea, an image of a form for the new work, emerges. When the idea arrives, it often does so suddenly and unexpectedly, as if coming from nowhere. I was puzzled about why, when this happens, I feel so elated, as if this were the perfect solution, even though I know from experience that sooner or later (and usually sooner) this elation will evaporate and the idea will seem at best flawed or at worst useless. It was clear to me from my own practice that making art involves inner processes, outside my awareness, operating in tandem with my interactions with the outside world, and I wanted to explore this further.

I wanted to trace the life story of new works of art from the moment of the artist's first inkling that she[1] is onto something to the completion of the work and its launch into the outside world. But it is generally recognised that artists are a particularly diverse set of individuals, each with their particular way of working, so I could not assume that my own experiences were shared by others. And perhaps other artists experienced states of mind that I did not. Indeed, it could be that each artist's process was so idiosyncratic that no common threads could be found. The way to test this out, of course, was to talk to other artists, and I set out to do this, beginning with the artists' group to which I belonged, and eventually conducting a formal qualitative research study involving interviews with 33 professional visual artists.[2] In these interviews, I was interested not only in what artists *do* as they make new works but also what they *feel*.

Although each artist had his or her own story to tell and the research revealed many differences between the processes of individual artists, there were also patterns in common. For instance, I found that my own experience of ideas bursting suddenly into consciousness was shared by many (but not all) the artists I interviewed. Others began work with their medium without a particular idea in mind and looked to the behaviour of the paint or other material to lead them to a subject for the work. I also found that, once they began work with their medium, artists' ideas of what they wanted to make would often change in response to the behaviour of their materials, so that they felt themselves to be involved in a dialogue with the medium out of which the form of the work gradually emerged. While working with their medium, many artists described being deeply absorbed in what some called a 'trance-like' state which must not be interrupted and which called for a contained physical space, such as a studio, and a boundaried space of time set apart from everyday life. Gradually, the developing work took on its final form, acquiring what many artists called its own 'life'. Once this life was established, the artist could let the work go into the outside world, and this separation seemed to be a relief for some artists and a painful wrench for others.

Some aspects of this emerging picture corresponded with expectations I had from thinking about my own process. But there were also new discoveries about the work of other artists and new realisations about my own process. I found that, for many of the artists I interviewed, each particular new artwork is triggered by an encounter with something in the outside world that seems to hold a personal significance. Although the artist might not be able to say what its significance is, this 'something' carries the promise that it could lead to a new artwork. I discuss this in Chapter 1, and I have called this experience of sensing the potential of something external the 'pre-sense'. At this point, though, the artist rarely has a clear idea of the form the potential artwork might take. A period of gestation in which nothing much seems to be happening is often necessary before a more specific idea of a form emerges. I consider this in detail in Chapters 2 and 3.

Chapter 4 goes on to consider the artist's relationship with her medium as she begins to translate her idea into a physical form. The interviews provided a great deal of evidence about how it feels to be in the process of making a work and the particular kind of concentration this involves. Artists spoke both about a state of deep involvement and about a focused attention that allows them to make moment to moment decisions about how to proceed. In Chapter 5, I introduce the terms 'extended self' and 'observer self' for these two states and discuss the ways in which artists experience them. Chapters 6 and 7 are also concerned with the stage of the artist's process when she is working with her medium. Several artists spoke of their work in terms of play, and Chapter 6 takes this up, whilst Chapter 7 links this to issues of creativity and destructiveness. Chapter 8 considers the space of the artwork and the external conditions the artist needs in order to work. From the interviews, it emerged that artists often find it difficult to enter their working state of mind, to leave their everyday concerns behind, and that they may need certain ritual procedures to help them to do this. This has led me to think in terms of an 'internal frame', peculiar to whichever medium the artist uses, that must be entered before work can begin. This concept is developed in Chapter 9.

As all the interviewees are professional artists, most of their artworks are destined for exhibitions or for delivery to commissioners. Often, a new work may lead directly to the next, and there may be clear connections between works in a series. But there may also be deep connections between seemingly disparate works made at different times, and these ongoing themes may only emerge when the artist looks back over a long period. Chapter 10 deals with the experience of finishing a work and letting it go into the outside world, and Chapter 11 with the connections between past, present and future works.

The choice of a chronological order for the book may be thought to imply that the events described in one chapter follow in time sequence from those in the previous one. This may be the case, but I do not want to suggest that the stages of making a new work always follow one another in a linear way. At any point, there may be a return to an earlier stage, and there may sometimes be many repetitions of a phase or series of phases before the work can proceed. In this sense, the trajectory of a work might be thought of as a spiral, rather than a straight, timeline.

The artist interviews, wonderfully articulate and even poetic as they often were, provided a great deal of new evidence, but they could never give the whole story. As many of the artists pointed out, the process of making art involves not only states of which we are aware and which we can describe but also processes outside our awareness about which we can say nothing. So, inevitably, there are crucial gaps in the evidence provided both by my own recording of my process and by the interviews. To think about these gaps, I have turned to psychoanalysis.

Freud himself wrote extensively about particular artworks but tended to focus on an analysis of the artwork and the motivation of the artist rather than the process of creating. Freud saw art as an example of sublimation, where sublimation is the unconscious transformation of socially unacceptable impulses (particularly sexual impulses) into a more socially acceptable form. Melanie Klein took a different view, seeing the making of art as an act of reparation – an attempt to repair damage done to the mother in phantasy by the baby in the earliest stages of life. Many interesting writers, including Hanna Segal, Adrian Stokes and Anton Ehrenzweig, have built on Klein's theories to develop their own ideas about the making of art. According to Freud and, in a different way, to Klein, artists are engaged in an attempt to deal with an inner conflict. That is, the primary motivation for making art is an internal problem. This view takes little account of the artwork as an object in itself that mirrors some aspect of the outside world. The interviews suggest that these artists are searching for a form that will embody their own personal and unique experience of being in the world. That is, the aspect of the outer world that has triggered the making of a particular work is of central importance, inextricably linked with their inner experience. My impression, from the artist interviews and from my own experience, is that the value of an artwork lies in its intertwining of outer and inner worlds, and that its making involves a continuous movement between the two.

One group of psychoanalytic writers, mostly from the British Independent tradition, speaks to this view. The psychoanalyst and paediatrician D.W. Winnicott regards creativity not as the prerogative of artists but as an essential aspect of healthy living, and he traces its roots to the earliest interactions between mother and baby. He questions the divide between personal inner fantasy and shared external 'reality' and introduces the concepts of 'potential space' and 'transitional phenomena' to refer to an area in which inner and outer worlds co-incide. This is a creative space that is rooted in infancy and continues throughout life in play and later in cultural experience. Marion Milner, a psychoanalyst, painter and writer, develops similar ideas in her writing about her own process of making art and has much to say about the artist's state of mind. In particular, she introduces the concept of 'illusion' to describe a fusion between inner and outer worlds, between the artist and the developing artwork, suggesting that this experience of 'oneness' is an essential step on the path to the creation of an artwork with a life of its own. The psychoanalyst Christopher Bollas also builds on Winnicott's work. He writes about the mother's transformational effect on the infant when the feed she offers transforms the baby's experience. In health, throughout life we continue this work of transformation by choosing objects and experiences that will develop our 'idiom' and the artist's activity is one particular way of furthering this development. In this theoretical frame, one that I adopt in this book, the artist's activity is neither regressive nor reparative but, rather, is an adult development of these early experiences. The making of art, then, is part of a lifelong process of self-realisation. It is also, at the same time, a means of offering a new view of some element of the external world.

The writing of this book has required a constant coming and going between the interviews, my own experience and the theory. I have searched out theoretical writing that might illuminate a particular aspect of the artists' experiences, or of my own, and then have returned to the interviews to check the extent to which the theory corresponds with artists' reported experiences. I have continually returned to the work of Winnicott, Milner and Bollas, together with other writers, to try to understand the inner processes that may underpin the artists' accounts of their experiences. As I had expected, there are many differences between the experiences of individual artists so that, in linking theory with evidence and looking for common threads, I also had to take account of these divergences. Gradually, I built up a narrative of the development of a new artwork. But some gaps remained. It seemed to me that existing psychoanalytic theory could not account for everything described by the interviewees or by myself. Where these gaps occurred, I have suggested new terms or extensions of theory to correspond with the evidence of the interviews.

At certain points in the book, I compare the processes of art-making to those of psychoanalysis. Looking back over the project as a whole, it seems that I have been engaged in the construction of a narrative of the life of artworks that parallels the construction of a patient's narrative in psychoanalysis. However, whilst the analyst is concerned with only one patient at a time, I have tried to trace both common ground and differences in the life histories of many artworks. In doing so, I have, inevitably, been influenced by my own experience as an artist. Whilst I have made every effort to take due account of artists' experiences that differ from my own, I may inadvertently have given more weight to those to which I could relate most readily. My findings may not apply to all artworks or to every artist, but I hope they will contribute to an ongoing debate.

We all experience the world in our own particular way. Everything we see is coloured by our inner lives. This book describes how artists create forms that embody their own personal experience of being in the world, forms in which the inner and the outer are inextricably intertwined. In doing so, they *both* present some aspect of the outside world in a new and unique way *and* further their own process of self-realisation.

Notes

1 Throughout the book, for simplicity, I use feminine pronouns when referring to artists of both sexes.
2 Twenty-five interviews are archived in the British Library Sound Archive. See the Appendix for more information.

1

THE PRE-SENSE

I find in everyday experience I cannot not be seduced by something at some point . . . I don't seek it out. I just experience life and it happens.

Laura Malacart

How does a new artwork come into being? Not surprisingly, the interviews with artists make it clear that there is no single answer to this question, and the issue of what constitutes the beginning of a new work is already complex. Each artist is influenced by her personal background, by her training, by previous work and by the cultural climate of her time, so that, in a sense, the artist's journey towards each work could be said to be life-long. For the purposes of this book, I have chosen to define the beginning as the point when the artist has a first intimation of the possibility of a new work. In this chapter, I examine my own experience and that of the artists I interviewed to trace the different ways in which the earliest stirrings of a potential in the mind of the artist may develop.

Among the artists I interviewed, many described an encounter with something in the outside world as usually marking their first awareness of the beginnings of a new work. One of the interviewees, Hayley Newman, describes her experience:

> *Generally, it kind of starts with a 'hunch' . . . just a sense of something that is interesting that is starting to engage me. [. . .] the 'hunch' is actually kind of a deliciously imaginative space. It's like the space that . . . I want to go to. Or something that triggers the imagination of a possibility in myself.*
>
> *(Newman 2011)*

The 'hunch' as a 'space' suggests an opening up, an expansion of the mind to allow many possibilities. The 'hunch' marks the beginning of an imaginative exploration of something that interests the artist, and Newman's description suggests that the interest is more than intellectual. It signals a personal engagement, and there is a sense of a process that has already begun. The 'hunch' is not a clear idea or image of a possible work. Such an image may or may not emerge later, but at this stage the lack of definition allows the artist space for her imagination to play unfettered by the restrictions of detail. The Oxford Online Dictionary gives the meaning of the noun 'hunch' as 'a feeling or guess based on intuition rather than fact' and lists 'feeling', 'impression', 'inkling', 'presentiment' and 'premonition' among its synonyms. The dictionary also lists informal synonyms as 'gut feeling' and 'feeling in one's bones'. All these terms may be relevant to the meaning that this artist gives to the word. By 'hunch', she is referring to a haptic experience that is felt in both body and mind.

The experience of finding something in the outside world that seems to have a special personal meaning and that promises the possibility of a new artwork was described by several of the interviewees:

> *I was in Pongee's the silk merchant buying some silk dupion for one project and found in their display racks . . . some tulle, some very light silk tulle in the perfect colour of the Chanel pink that I use a lot. And I bought my silk dupion at vast expense, but in my mind was the silk tulle, what could I do with it.*
>
> (Kivland 2011)

> *I just came across a photograph that I hadn't seen before recently of a woman on the shore near where we are . . . and there's something in the photograph that . . . not quite sure what it is, and it's quite, it's not very clear, it's quite a blurred photograph, but there's something about it that appeals to me as a painter.*
>
> (O'Donoghue 2013)

In one sense, these two experiences are rather different from one another. Sharon Kivland sees some material that she wants to use as a *medium* for an artwork whereas Hughie O'Donoghue sees a photograph that may offer a new *subject* for a painting. But there are also factors in common. For both artists, the discovery of something in the outside world has triggered an imaginative response. It has set off an internal process that may eventually result in a new work. An important point seems to be that there is a certain vagueness or openness in the artist's experience at this point. Kivland's fascination with the silk tulle is related to its sensual qualities — its lightness and its pink colour — but she does not yet know where this will take her. For O'Donoghue, the indistinctness of the image is important in that the photograph does not tie itself too specifically to a particular woman. I will use the term 'pre-sense' to denote the initial sense of something that is of personal interest, that engages the artist's imagination, inviting further exploration and offering the possibility of a new work. (In previous publications, such as Townsend (2015, 2017), I have used the term 'hunch' for this experience.) In this chapter, I explore the nature of this pre-sense, the various ways in which it may emerge and the ways in which it may be developed by the artist.

In order to explore this in more depth, I will give an account of my own experience of beginning a new series of artworks:

> *Some years ago I began to spend regular periods of time in the Lake District in North-West England. Much of my artwork relates to landscape and my intention was to make artworks responding to some aspect of this area. But despite, or perhaps because of, the beauty of my surroundings, I could find no subject to capture my imagination. I was staying in a valley halfway between the mountains and Morecambe Bay, a vast expanse of quicksands, channels and intertidal mudflats. After a while I noticed that I would always travel to the mountains rather than to the coastline. The mountains attracted me. They seemed to me to be comforting, solid, dependable, containing. The Bay, on the other hand, seemed too open, too flat, too vast. There was something troubling about this landscape. Was it the history of the Bay, the fact that many lives have been lost here to the quicksands or to fast incoming tides? Looking out over the great expanse of the Bay at low tide, I imagined myself walking out alone towards the horizon until I could see no land. I imagined what it might feel like to be out in this wet desert, far from help. This sense of isolation and lack of containment seemed to be one aspect of my emotional reaction to the Bay. Another had to do with the imagined experience of being sucked beneath the ground by quicksands. Or being swept away, engulfed, by the incoming tide which is said to be as fast as a galloping horse. But I felt that there was more to my feelings about the Bay than these emotionally charged images. It was as if these reactions were the tip of an iceberg and that below the surface were less conscious associations, which I could not yet access. It was this feeling that propelled me to make a series of artworks related to the Bay.[1]*

Something about the Bay resonated with something in me, leaving me with the sense that something significant was going on. This also seemed to offer the promise that the Bay might provide the means to find a form (in the shape of a new artwork) for this experience. There was a felt sense that here in the outer world was a perceptual form that chimed with the inner. There was not an exact fit between inner and outer, but there was the promise that some sort of fit could be found in the form of an artwork.

In retrospect, it seemed that I had been alert for some aspect or element of the landscape which would evoke a particular sort of emotional response. The mountains appealed strongly to me, but I was not drawn to make art related to them. Rather, it seems that I was, without being fully aware of it at the time, seeking something that would arouse a more ambivalent reaction. The Bay was troubling and so offered the possibility of making a work that might clarify this uneasy response. It raised my anxieties, and the possibility of creating a series of works related to it was both exciting and fearful because I knew that, in doing so, I would be stepping into unknown territory, exploring something that I did not yet understand and that might uncover painful or even terrifying emotions.

Kivland's fascination with the silk tulle, O'Donoghue's 'something that appeals', Newman's 'hunch' and my own response to Morecambe Bay all signal a resonance between inner and outer worlds. It is this resonance, together with the artist's presentiment that she will be able to create an artwork related to this sensation, that constitutes the experience that I call the 'pre-sense'. The artist has the sense of something significant that cannot yet be apprehended clearly.

I want to think about the nature of this resonance between inner and outer by bringing in the writing of the psychoanalyst and paediatrician D.W. Winnicott on transitional objects and transitional phenomena. Winnicott observed that, as the infant begins to move towards objective perception based on reality testing, he[2] may adopt a teddy bear, piece of blanket or other item that assumes great significance, particularly at moments of separation or anxiety. The bear or blanket is a substitute for the missing sensory elements of the mother's body and offers the child a form to correspond to his need. Winnicott suggests that these 'transitional objects', along with other 'transitional phenomena' (for instance, for the infant, such activities as babbling or rhythmic movements leading to sleep), belong to both inner and outer reality simultaneously. In a radical departure from earlier classical psychoanalytic theory, Winnicott postulates an intermediate area of experiencing, a potential space, between the world of shared external reality and the personal inner world (Winnicott 1953). It is a space of illusion in which objects have both an autonomous external existence and a life in the inner world of the individual. Through the concept of transitional phenomena, Winnicott links the early experiences of the infant, who creates a personal 'transitional object', with the play of the older child and with cultural experience in adult life. All these situations take one into 'an area that is not challenged, because no claim is made on its behalf except that it shall exist as a resting place for the individual engaged in the perpetual human task of keeping inner and outer reality separate yet interrelated' (ibid.: 3).

My encounter with Morecambe Bay, Kivland's discovery of the silk tulle and O'Donoghue's finding of the photograph can all be understood in terms of transitional phenomena. When I responded emotionally to the landscape of Morecambe Bay, I was in a state of mind in which the outer reality of the landscape affected me and, at the same time, I projected my own feelings and memories and fantasies onto the landscape. I imbued the Bay with my own personal meaning (though this meaning was not yet articulated). The boundaries between me and the landscape were partially dissolved so that I could no longer say whether my perceptions were of outer reality or of my own inner world. They were both at the same moment.

Winnicott does not discuss the artist's activity in any detail, but he does write about his view of the origins of creativity in the earliest stages of life. He describes the situation in which the infant is searching for 'something', having a sense or intimation of something that will correspond to his need but not yet knowing what form this 'something' will take. The mother's response, in offering her breast, provides a form that fits the infant's intimation. According to Winnicott, if the infant imagines (or hallucinates) the breast at the moment when his mother presents it to him, the infant has the illusion that he has created the breast. Winnicott terms this experience 'primary creativity'. This is the precursor to the stage of the transitional object. Whilst the experience of primary creativity is facilitated by the mother's presenting *herself* to the infant, the infant 'discovers' the transitional object (an object that is 'not me' and also 'not mother') for himself. These early experiences form the basis of creative activity in adulthood where creative living is understood as endowing elements of the outside world with a personal meaning. Winnicott specifically mentions the arts as a potential area of transitional phenomena (and therefore of creative living) for the audience (Winnicott 1953: 16).

The artist's creation of an artwork follows in a direct line from the infant's 'creation' of the breast, through the use of a transitional object and the older child's play. In all these activities, something in the outside world provides an external form for something from the inner world through a process that involves an overlap between inner and outer. In primary creativity, the mother's response in presenting her breast to her baby at the right moment gives form to the infant's preconception that there is something to be found that will satisfy him. The transitional object gives form to the infant's sense of missing the mother's physical presence. The artist too has an intimation (a pre-sense) that there is something to be found or, rather, created that will correspond with an inner experience (whether or not she eventually succeeds in creating such a form). But there is a difference between the artist's situation and the interaction between inner and outer in the infant's 'creation' of the breast or his use of the transitional object. The infant finds the breast and the transitional object ready made. No physical transformation of the external object is necessary (although there is a psychic transformation). The artist, on the other hand, must create her own form. There is a closer parallel between artist and the older child at play, as the child may build his own world, reflecting his inner landscape, through his use of toys or other materials. Of course, this is not to say that art practice is equivalent to child's play. Art is made within a cultural context, drawing on a cultural heritage and usually with the intention of presenting the finished work to an audience.

But although Winnicott's writing on the origins of creativity and on transitional phenomena is helpful in thinking about my experience of Morecambe Bay, it does not fully explain the state of mind that accompanies the 'pre-sense'. The endowing of something in the outside world with personal meaning is not something peculiar to artists. As Winnicott says, it is the hallmark of creative living for everyone. But for the artist, there is something more to this experience on those occasions when it gives rise to the desire to make an artwork.

So what is this 'something more'? The baby's hallucination of the breast and the use of a transitional object are essentially physical, bodily experiences. The artist interviews indicate that the pre-sense also has a physical component. Henrietta Simson says of the subject of her painting:

It's almost like kind of wanting to be closer to the thing somehow than just visually.
If you can take it and recreate it as your own . . . it's a closer connection somehow.
It's not just a kind of visual thing any more . . . . grabbing it in a stronger way than
just looking at it maybe.

(Simson 2011)

Simson's experience of the 'thing' in the outside world is of being drawn to it
in a haptic, bodily way. 'Just looking' implies a distance between viewer and
whatever is viewed, but this artist seems to want to get inside the 'thing' or to
have it inside her, and only through this experience can she 'recreate it as [her]
own'. In a similar vein, the photographer Susan Derges, speaking about her work
River Taw, says 'The ideas behind the project were about becoming close to the
element of the river, as a metaphor of immersion and participation. I was looking
to be part of it . . .' (Read 2017: 116).

The psychoanalyst and artist Marion Milner seems to be exploring a similar experience when she writes about the bodily nature of her response to her
subject matter. She writes about the difficulty of preserving her experience in
her painting and comes to feel that she needs to 'spiritually envelop' her subject
before starting work. She quotes a passage from a diary note:

The impulse to paint those flowers, crimson cyclamen, feels like a desire
to perpetuate the momentary glimpse of timeless peace that is given by the
extension of their petals in space. I want to taste it continually, swallow it,
become merged with it – just like those feelings of wanting to eat a landscape, or having eaten it; as if there was an equal expense of space inside
one, a sort of through-the-looking-glass land.

(Milner 1957: 57)

Milner's experience of the flowers is visual, kinaesthetic and gustatory.
Although Milner calls this 'spiritual envelopment', the metaphor of eating makes
it clear that, for Milner, this is a very visceral experience. She wants to incorpo-
rate the flowers in order to become 'merged' with them, and she regards this act
of taking in as a necessary step on the path to making a painting. The painting is
intended to preserve the artist's experience, putting it (or, rather, a transformed
version of it) back into the outside world. For Milner herself, this act of taking
in is fraught with anxiety because she does not know whether she will be able
to create a satisfactory painting. If not, she may feel that 'by having it inside one
might have destroyed it'. She speculates that 'To an established painter, who
knows that he can successfully bring what he has taken inside himself back to life
in the outside world as a painting, there may be less anxiety in this act of spiritual
envelopment' (Milner 1957: 63).

Milner's description suggests that the beginning of a new work of art is heralded by the *taking in* of something from the outside world and she, like Derges
and Simson, wishes to merge with her subject matter. Milner says of her own

desire to paint: 'I wanted to ensoul nature with what was really there, to make perception of the hidden insides and essential nature of objects fit in with what I knew, in moments of keenest awareness, to be really there' (Milner 1957: 120). She writes of the 'soul' of her subject: '. . . a "soul" which was both really there, but which also was something that I had given to it from my own memory and feeling, since otherwise I would not have been able to see what was really there' (ibid.). Milner insists that she perceives a hidden something in nature that 'really' exists and that it is essential to the object she wants to paint: it is its 'soul'. But this 'soul' can only be perceived by Milner through her endowment of the object with elements of her own inner world. In other words, this 'soul' belongs not only to 'nature' but to herself. Milner's use of the word 'soul', and her writing about wanting to 'spiritually envelop' her subject, are examples of her trying to find a way of describing an experience that does not easily lend itself to everyday language. At times, she seems to write of the artist's experience in similar terms to meditative practice in which there may be a loss of awareness of personal boundaries. She writes that (provided one's separate body identity has already been established): 'the demarcation of the boundaries of one's spiritual identity are not fixed, they do not have to remain identical with one's skin' (ibid.: 143). In relation to the artist's experience of whatever element in the outside world she responds to, Milner seems to suggest that the artist's 'spiritual identity' expands to include that element.

There is a difference between Milner's formulation of the artist's experience and Winnicott's theory of transitional phenomena. Transitional phenomena hark back to the developmental phase when the infant is beginning to have a sense of separateness from his mother, whereas Milner's descriptions relate more closely to an earlier stage. That is, Milner's writing compares the artist's experience with the very early relationship between mother and infant when the infant does not yet experience him- or herself as separate from the mother (or primary caregiver). Winnicott, in writing about transitional phenomena, is concerned with the slightly later stage when the infant begins to discover that the mother (or caregiver) is a person in her own right.

In my own art practice, I think that the initial realisation that I have found something 'out there' that resonates with something inner and that can lead me to a new artwork can be accompanied by a temporary sense of at-oneness with the potential subject matter. It is as if this outside something is no longer outside but has become an integral part of my sense of myself. In Milner's terms, I have taken the outside something into myself. Christopher Bollas, a psychoanalyst who develops Winnicott's ideas and is also influenced by Milner, uses the term 'aesthetic moment' for experiences such as these which 'crystallise time into a space where subject and object appear to achieve an intimate rendezvous' (Bollas 2018: 15–16). Bollas' description of the aesthetic moment is closely tied in with his concept of the transformational object. Bollas builds on Winnicott's ideas to emphasise the transformational effect the mother has on her infant. He writes:

If he [the infant] is distressed, the resolution of discomfort is achieved by the apparition-like presence of mother. The pain of hunger, a moment of emptiness, is transformed by mother's milk into an experience of fullness. This is primary transformation: emptiness, agony and rage become fullness and content. The aesthetic of this experience is the particular way the mother meets the infant's need and transforms his internal and external realities.

(Bollas 2018: 17)

Here, Bollas links the concept of the aesthetic with the infant's earliest experiences of transformation by the actions of his mother. He writes: 'The mother's idiom of care and the infant's experience of this handling is one of the first if not the earliest human aesthetic. It is the most profound occasion when the nature of the self is formed and transformed by the environment' (ibid.: 17). That is, Bollas equates the aesthetic with a process of transformation of the self brought about by something or someone (initially the mother) in the outside world (although at the very early stage of life Bollas refers to above, the infant himself has not yet made a reliable distinction between inside and outside). In Bollas' view, all later aesthetic experiences, whether of art, music, literature or landscape, are existential recollections of these early moments. Throughout life, he suggests, we both search out and come across 'transformational objects' that will further our self-development. He writes: 'The transformational object seems to offer the beseeching subject an experience where self fragmentations will be integrated through a processing form' (ibid.: 17). This 'processing form' harks back to the experience of the mother as processing the infant's experience, whilst the adjective 'beseeching' invokes the sense of a desire or urgent need for the transformational object. Both Bollas and Winnicott, then, see the earliest interaction of mother and infant as forming the basis for future self-development. Winnicott frames this in terms of creativity, whilst Bollas focuses on aesthetic experience and the search for transformation. For the artist, and perhaps for everyone, these concepts are closely interlinked.

The outside something that catches the artist's attention and gives rise to a pre-sense is already a 'transformational object' for the artist. At the moment when Kivland finds her silk or O'Donoghue finds his photograph, or the landscape of Morecambe Bay resonates with something inner for me, the silk or the photograph or the Bay expands the artist's experience. Bollas writes: 'we are played upon by the inspiring arrival of the unselected . . . It opens us up, liberating an area like a key fitting a lock. In such moments we can say that objects use us' (Bollas 1992a: 37). The metaphor of a key fitting a lock and opening a door seems to me to speak both to the sense of a 'fit' between the outside something and inner experience and to the sense that inner experience is released as it spreads out into the object. The idea that such objects 'use' us as well as our using them speaks to a deep and dynamic connection between the artist and the object. The outside something is already transforming the artist's experience and there is a sense that something significant is happening. At this point, the experience is personal to the artist. Others are unlikely to respond to these particular elements of the outside world with the same intensity. But the artist senses a potential to create an artwork, a new form that will be available to others. This new form may become a transformational object for an audience. The intimation of a potential to create a transformational object both for herself and for others is the artist's pre-sense.

The aesthetic moment, as described by Bollas, is a momentary glimpse. The sense of oneness does not last for long. For the artist who has a pre-sense, the aesthetic moment, if it occurs, is succeeded by an interaction between inner and outer that is not so much a momentary state of mind as an ongoing process. Here, Winnicott's ideas about transitional phenomena are pertinent. Transitional phenomena relate to a transition in time – a movement from the experience of the other as a subjective object to the experience of the other as an object with a separate existence. For the artist, this transition includes the gradual sorting out of the elements in the outside something that are essential to the pre-sense – those elements that chime with something inner – from those that are superfluous to it. Marion Milner writes 'it was necessary to select those details of appearances which emphasised the nature of the "soul" of what I was looking at' (Milner 1957: 120). She wants her painting to convey something of her own response, and this will be done through the 'details of appearances' that *she* feels capture the essence of the scene. In making the moving image installation *Under the Skin*, I wanted to create an artwork that would convey something of my experience of Morecambe Bay as an expanse of living sands – treacherous, unstable, potentially overwhelming and yet enticing. In order to do so, I had to find elements in the landscape that I could use to construct a work that might encompass these different qualities. These elements were the very ones that had first affected me and given rise to my pre-sense. They were as much a part of my own inner world as they were present in the Bay.

Milner's selection of the essential 'details of appearances' and my own selection of aspects of the Bay are processes of abstraction. Susanne Langer (1942, 1953), a philosopher whose work influenced Milner, developed a theory of symbolisation, differentiating between the discursive symbols of language that *describe* whatever is symbolised, and presentational symbols of art which *show* the viewer what a particular area of emotional life is like. According to Langer, abstraction is an essential feature of symbolisation. Considering the making of art, she writes of 'the paramount importance of *abstracting the form*, banning all irrelevancies that might obscure its logic, and especially divesting it of all its usual meanings so it may be open to new ones' (Langer 1953: 59–60). Anything that ties it to 'worldly offices' is dispensed with so that only those features that are relevant to the artist's experience are retained. Milner also came to see the artist as engaged in a process of symbolisation whereby the artwork symbolises something about the inner life of the artist. She writes: 'I could look on the artist as creating symbols for the life of feeling, creating ways in which the inner life may be made knowable; which, as Freud said, can only be done in terms of the outer life' (Milner 1987: 226). It is usually the artist's experience of something in the outer world that sets the process of making a new work in motion and the new work will offer a form for something previously unformed or unknown in the artist's inner life. Because this is achieved 'in terms of the outer life', the artwork will not only make the inner world more 'knowable' but also shed new light on an aspect of the outer world.

Milner insists that she is painting what is 'really there'. Langer seems to describe a similar situation when she discusses Paul Cézanne's reflections on his work. She writes 'the translation of natural objects into pictorial elements took place *in his seeing*, in the act of looking, not the act of painting. Therefore, in recording what he saw he earnestly believed that he painted exactly what "was there"' (Langer 1953: 78). Langer's emphasis on the act of looking introduces a further factor into the situation. I have considered the way in which the artist responds emotionally to whatever it is in the outside world that has captured her interest, and this response colours her perception. But her perception, the way in which she *sees*, is also affected by the medium she uses. When I worked as a photographer making montaged black-and-white photographs in the darkroom, I found myself seeing the world around me as if through the lens of my camera. I noticed differences in tone and texture rather than colour, and I was aware of shapes that might or might not lend themselves to the montage process. More recently, I have come to work mainly with the moving image, usually in colour, and I find that I am no longer so acutely aware of tones and textures. Instead I am more focused on movement and colour. My very perception of the outside world is conditioned by the way I work. That is, the artist's process of form-making or symbolisation starts from the moment she encounters something in the outside world that resonates with something inner. At that moment, she is already abstracting those details that are pertinent to her medium and that she could use in her work.

Sometimes the interaction between inner and outer worlds may not only give rise to a desire to make a new work but may compel the artist to try to do so. A way must somehow be found. Something important to the artist is at stake. As one of the interviewees, Laura Malacart, says: 'There's an urgency . . . the situation must be dealt with.' The art historian Michael Podro writes of 'the sense of urgency that drives the making of any work of art, the existential urgency springing from the need to be a participant and not a bystander of one's own world' (Podro 2007: 31). Podro's statement links with Winnicott's writing on transitional phenomena and his view of creativity as the endowing of the external world with one's inner life. But there is sometimes more to the felt sense of urgency. If the artwork is to provide a form for something previously unformed or unknown in the artist's inner experience, then the urgency may be understood in terms of a pressure towards meaning and coherence.

I recall an incident that gave rise to a compelling sense of urgency in me. Many years ago, shortly after I had taken up photography and was in the initial stages of training as a psychoanalytic psychotherapist, I took part in a training group that was being observed through a one-way mirror. There was an incident in the group that aroused strong emotions in me. I could find no words for my feelings but an image came into my mind of a figure inside a transparent egg-shaped form. I felt impelled to make a photograph of this image. Photoshop had not yet been invented and I had never tried to construct montaged images in the darkroom, but I felt I must teach myself to do so. I succeeded in producing an image that was a close enough fit for my feeling, and I found that the photograph itself provided a container for my experience. The incident in the group, and the presence of the unseen observers, had stirred up emotions that were not yet articulated and my task in making the photograph was to find a form for them. The resulting photograph seemed to help me to process my feelings *without necessarily giving them verbal expression*. In this case, the initial stage of the 'pre-sense' (that is, the feelings aroused by the incident in the group) led directly and rapidly to a specific idea for an image that would provide a form for the experience. More usually, there are intermediate stages.

Once the artist has found her subject matter, her task is to create a form that reflects her inner experience and correlates with the initial sense of significance she experienced in her encounter with something external. The analysis of the artist interviews suggests that there are two possible trajectories. Some artists go straight from here to an engagement with their medium. Through this engagement, the new form will gradually emerge. I discuss this stage of the process in Chapter 4. Other artists move towards a more specific idea (that is, a mental image, which may be more or less vague, of a potential form for the final work) by beginning to research their subject, try out sketches or make other preparations. I discuss this in the next chapter.

Notes

1 This is an extract from my own process diaries. Other quotations from these diaries appear throughout the book. Some of these extracts also appear in the chapter 'Making Space' in *Little Madnesses: Winnicott, Transitional Phenomena and Cultural Experience* (Townsend 2013).

2 I will use the masculine pronoun when referring to the child in order to differentiate from references to the mother.

2

PREPARATION, RESEARCH AND GESTATION

It comes together in a semi-subconscious way. I think it's about all the stuff you put in beforehand and then, in this fabulous, wonderful way, something links up.

Edward Allington

Once they have found their subject matter, some artists described a period of preparation or research intended to lead them towards an idea for the new work. This preparation is the artist's attempt to clarify the pre-sense. As Hayley Newman says: 'And then, then I kind of follow through, I kind of follow-up on those hunches and start researching I guess. So I start to look at the subject I'm interested in.'

After I had decided to make a work related to Morecambe Bay but before I had lighted on an idea for a particular work, I began to experiment with photography and video:

Initially, I had no idea how I might approach the subject beyond the fact that my usual media are video, photography and installation. I spent long periods of time traversing the coastline and finding positions or vantage points that seemed 'right'. I could not necessarily say what was right about them. One favourite area at the mouth of an estuary had a small pier from which I could film the incoming tide. Another spot had deep channels in the sand that altered with every tide. I took many photographs and shot many hours of video footage in an attempt to clarify what it was that I wanted to make.

In this period of preparation, I was looking for something that 'felt right', something in the landscape of Morecambe Bay that would give form to my inner experience. Through my repeated visits to the Bay, I became familiar with the movement of the tides, the changing of the channels on the beach, the effects of the weather and so on. I was also attempting to come to a deeper understanding of the way these elements in the outside world affected me emotionally (of course, I could only come to a deeper understanding of those aspects of my experience that were available to consciousness. There was also a level of unconscious meaning that was not accessible.) At the same time, my photographs and videos were attempts to work towards a form for the final work that would satisfy me visually. These elements were closely intertwined in that the visual satisfaction I sought would largely (but not only) have to do with the ability of the photographs or films to embody my experience. In addition, the final work had to have the visual qualities that, in my opinion, would allow it to become a sufficiently strong work within my own artistic practice.

Having decided on his subject area, Hughie O'Donoghue describes the next stage of his process:

> *Artists traditionally use drawing to inform their practice. They sit down and draw things and look at them intently. I don't do that, it's not how I work, but I look at things intently. And so when a subject emerges I tend to read around the subject and try and get some sort of feeling for the subject. Because in order to make a painting about something you really need to know the subject inside out. This sort of immersing yourself in the subject is almost like a process of preparation for something that might happen.*
>
> *(O'Donoghue 2013)*

This artist has already found a 'subject' that combines elements of the outer world with elements of his own inner experience. His 'immersion in the subject' is a deeper exploration of the overlap between these elements as his choice of reading matter is determined by his personal areas of interest. He is not only looking for information but also exploring his own emotional responses. 'Immersing' is an evocative word suggesting a transition from one element to another. The implication is that he enters the realm of his subject so that he can know it from the inside. This is an interesting reversal of the imagery used by Milner in the passage I quote in the previous chapter in which she describes her initial interaction with the subject of her painting. She writes of the 'taking in' of something external. Here, at a slightly later stage of his process, O'Donoghue sees himself as immersed in (or taken in by) something external, the wider ramifications of his 'subject'. This suggests an initial taking in of some element of the outside world, with an accompanying pre-sense that then acts as a guide as the artist becomes immersed in an exploration of the subject. I think that this spatial metaphor is helpful in considering the progression of the artist's process, but too literal a division between the concepts of 'taking in' and 'being taken in by' could be misleading. The imagery used both by O'Donoghue and by Milner conveys a sense that the boundaries between the external and the internal are permeable. Here, I think that Winnicott's writing on transitional phenomena is relevant. In describing an area of experience in which inner and outer worlds co-incide, Winnicott used several different terms, including 'intermediate area' and 'potential space'. The encounter between O'Donoghue and his wider 'subject' can be considered to be taking place within a potential space where his perceptions of the 'subject' become inextricably mixed with his emotional responses. At this point in his process, he seems actively to choose to enter this space in order to immerse himself in his subject. O'Donoghue speaks of his research as a preparation for 'something that might happen', something not within his conscious control, perhaps anticipating the later stage of illumination in which an idea may emerge.

The artist and photographer Susan Derges describes the early stages of her work:

> The idea is never clear at the outset. I don't begin with a totally clarified concept but more of an intuition of something that I'm trying to articulate. It is *sensed*; the territory of it is defined but not completely distinct. So, the process of researching or investigating an idea, which I use as a method of testing the idea, is the process by which the nature of that idea becomes clearer to me. The research will disprove some of it and back up other parts, fleshing it out in surprising ways. The process of research is part and parcel of an idea coming into full fruition or formation.
>
> *(Derges in Read 2017: 117)*

Derges uses the term 'idea' in different ways here. At the beginning of the passage, she uses it to refer to an area of interest that is not yet elucidated. This is what I am calling the 'pre-sense'. Her research begins the process of elucidation and the developed idea in 'full fruition or formation' is what I refer to in this chapter as the 'idea'. The movement from pre-sense to idea involves a testing of the pre-sense both through contextual and theoretical research and through a speculative or tentative engagement with her medium. She goes on to clarify her use of the term 'intuition':

> There has to be an intuition first, otherwise the research gives you nothing. It has to be led by the intimation of an idea but one must be prepared for the research to take you into the unknown and away from it, in order to bring you back to it again in a stronger more amazing manifestation.
>
> *(Read 2017: 118)*

Derges links her intuition with the 'intimation of an idea', or, as I call it in this book, her pre-sense. Intuition is essential in guiding her research, leading her towards elements that elucidate the pre-sense and paving the way for the advent of a more specific idea. Interestingly, she implies that the artist must be prepared not only to go into the unknown but also to move away from the pre-sense at least temporarily. In attempting to understand what this might mean in the context of my own work, I find that I must be prepared to let go of any pre-conceptions of what form the emerging idea might eventually take. The process of research brings me back to the pre-sense, as Derges describes, but in unexpected ways.

Christopher Bollas relates the process of unconscious data collection to intuition. He suggests that the accumulated experiences of the artist or scientist as he develops his creative work result in an 'increasingly specific vision of his object world':

> What is this ability that derives from the incremental cohesion of a mental structure set up to think an as yet inarticulated idea? Is this not what we mean by a sense of intuition: the sense we have of where to look, what to look at, and how to look at it?
>
> *(Bollas 1992b: 89)*

According to Bollas, intuition is an unconscious skill that allows the creative person both to know where to look in the outside world to find those elements that will contribute to his or her personal development and also to know 'how to receive messages (or significations)' (ibid.: 91). This formulation gives appropriate weight to the long experience that lies behind the birth of each new artwork. As an interviewee, Jo Volley, says: 'I think all that intuition is just years and years of experience and ideas mulling around that you're not necessarily all that kind of conscious of.' And Hughie O'Donoghue puts it this way: 'As an artist you carry with you your own history of what you've already done, you know, the paintings you've already made.' In a sense, the artist has gone through a training in intuition so that her perceptions are increasingly refined and increasingly attuned to responding to elements which will carry her work forward.

Gina Glover, a photographer, describes how she searches for the image she needs:

> *Right at the beginning of a piece of work I might have a very vague idea of what I might be interested in. . . . I am always collecting images that at some point I may pull out and it may become a piece of work.*
>
> *(Glover 2011)*

Glover's playful collecting of images, led by her intuition, allows her to pick out any that might take her work forward. Other artists may discover relevant items in different ways. O'Donoghue came across glass plate negatives in a shop:

> *I'm often asked 'well that's really strange . . . you're fortunate to be in the right place at the right time', or 'you found those glass plate negatives, that's incredibly lucky'. It actually isn't, you've either got your antennae up or not. So things happen.*
>
> *(O'Donoghue 2013)*

O'Donoghue's use of the metaphor of antennae suggests a picking up of messages from the outside world that are relevant to his particular preoccupations. This process seems to relate to Bollas' description of intuition. But Bollas writes of intuition as an unconscious skill. Considering O'Donoghue's description in the light of Bollas' definition, the roots of his 'antennae' are in the unconscious and their function is to connect his unconscious concerns with elements in the outside world. He was not actively looking for the glass plate negatives but, when he saw them, he knew, through intuition, that they were relevant to his project.

The elements that seem relevant may be physical objects, such as the glass plate negatives, or intangible data such as thoughts or ideas that are stored mentally, as Russell Mills describes:

> *I have a certain set of ideas in my head – passions that I want to explore. So you're constantly looking for things that connect – that have some correspondence to those ideas . . . It's what I call shed mentality . . . to be so curious about the world that you absorb all these diverse ideas and then somehow make something new out of them.*
>
> *(Mills 2011)*

At this preparation stage, guided by intuition, Mills collects both mental and physical data relevant to his pre-sense of new works. His 'mental shed' acts as an internal contained space within which these elements can connect and interact. He says that he 'somehow' makes something new out of them, indicating that this interaction takes place, at least partially, outside his awareness.

Bollas stresses the fact that the intuiting person is unaware of what he is working on. He has not yet 'thought' it, and therefore it is protected from the possible judgements of consciousness: 'the intuiting person is unconsciously able to explore lines of investigation that would meet with incredulous disapproval if he were fully conscious of what was being considered' (Bollas 1992b: 92). For the artist, this lack of awareness is not about the subject matter of the work. For instance, O'Donoghue knows that his subject matter is his father's letters. However, he does not know how the elements he finds through his research and intuitive searching will combine and interact. This combination and interaction takes place out of the artist's awareness. The artist continues in the hope and expectation that, from this interaction, an idea or image for a new artwork will emerge, but he cannot predict what this idea will be or when it will present itself.

The artist's preparation through research, introspection and exploration of possible forms (either through practical trials in drawings, taking photographs, collecting objects or by imaginative explorations) may result in the gradual emergence of a specific direction or idea for a new work. However, a new idea may not be forthcoming at first. Many artists described a time gap between their initial interest in a particular subject and the eventual emergence of the idea for a work. Artists Jon Thomson and Alison Craighead, who work together, say:

> *There is a push and pull, I think, as well where we'll talk about something and we won't really get anywhere and then you sleep on it and you suddenly take a step forward and so it sort of comes in cycles.*
>
> *(Thomson and Craighead 2011)*

Thomson and Craighead describe an integral aspect of their process, suggesting that their ideas for each work progress as a series of discrete steps. Their description points up the cyclical nature of the process, with short periods of 'gestation' occurring overnight and leading to onward steps. However, the arrival of the 'step forward' is not predictable. Sometimes they need to wait, as Craighead explains:

> So it's going from having this initial thing or interest to it being at a point where it might start to become more. There is a space between those two points and that's the grumpy bit, potentially.
>
> *(ibid.)*

If the time gap before a way forward emerges is a long one, this stage of the work can be frustrating, as I describe:

> After I had taken many photographs and shot many hours of video there came a long period when I felt that nothing was happening, that I had no ideas. No new images came to me. I felt stuck and frustrated, not knowing how to proceed.

This potential 'grumpiness' or frustration arises out of the fear that no way forward will present itself and that the artist will be marooned in this uncomfortable waiting state. In the gap between the point of initial interest and 'something more', the artist has to let go, to relinquish control without knowing what, if anything, will emerge.

For some artists, the time gap between initial interest and specific idea is very protracted:

> It's come back. You'd visualised it maybe ten years ago but it didn't make sense at the time. I think the idea has been smouldering away. That little drawing . . . It's become an idea by bursting into flame.
>
> *(Aiken 2011)*

> It did come in a flash. I do get that occasionally . . . these flashes . . . things at the corner of your mind as well as your eye . . . I do mull over things a lot. I do ruminate. They're with me for a very long time and mostly sketchbook scribbles rather than planned drawings of these things.
>
> *(Volley 2011)*

Aiken's and Volley's descriptions are of more infrequent events, and it was only in retrospect that they could view the delay as signalling a period of gestation. They had not been working consciously on the problem for some time but had left it aside. Both Aiken and Volley suggest that, prior to the flash of insight or inspiration, something had been 'smouldering away' or was being mulled over at a level below full consciousness. In Aiken's case, a visualisation of a possible work, in abeyance for ten years, has been revivified, and he now sees it in a new way. The word 'smouldering' suggests a very active and transformative process.

It seems that, out of the artist's awareness, the previous visualisation has been linked to something new, causing it to 'burst into flame', a description that captures something of the intensity of the experience. But this ignition only occurs after an extended unconscious process that might be thought of as incubation or gestation, a period during which new links are made and a new idea is formed. As Russell Mills says:

> Generally this work takes place over quite a long period of time and sometimes I get kind of lost . . . I don't know where it's going and I don't know what to do with it. I don't really dwell on it too much initially. I just put it away, I just kind of surrender . . . maybe it's redundant, maybe it's a bad idea . . . I just put it away and do something else . . . Eventually, something else will happen, something else will come along, another trigger will come to be the hook I need to make this connection with what I was working on. This little chain link appears: 'Oh yeah! Of course, that's the way to go' . . . I would say that in retrospect all the work I've done has had a period of gestation.
>
> (Mills 2011)

Mills' description is not of the emergence of an initial idea for a new piece of work but of periodic hitches in an ongoing work when a new direction is called for to propel the work forward. When Mills does not know what to do with the work, he puts it aside, but he seems to do this in an open-minded way. He does not see himself as faced with the decision as to whether to abandon this route or whether to continue with it. He recognises that it may need a period of gestation until an external 'trigger' connects with it to generate a new idea. Susan Collins describes her experience of moving towards an idea for a work:

> I think it's more like a marrying one thing with another but sometimes things do just 'ping' . . . but you do have to have the conditions for the ping . . . Sometimes you can research everything really, really thoroughly and get terribly bogged down and the whole thing can get a bit worthy . . . then you've got to leave those things aside and something can appear to come from nowhere but actually what's happening is something has been processed in the back of your head.
>
> (Collins 2014)

Collins recognises that ideas emerge through the linking of apparently disparate elements. Sometimes this 'marrying' is not achieved by research and conscious effort. The 'ping' of a new idea may come only after she has left the work aside for a while to allow it to gestate out of her awareness.

The artists' descriptions of periods of gestation suggest the presence of an internal protected space where thoughts, perceptions, feelings, fantasies and memories related to the work can be stored in abeyance and where a process of linking can take place. Christopher Bollas introduces the concept of the 'receptive unconscious' (Bollas 1992b), which can be understood as just such an internal space. To develop his theory of the receptive unconscious, Bollas starts from

Freud's writing on repression. According to Freud, instincts and memories that would cause intolerable anxiety if allowed to enter consciousness are banished to the repressed unconscious. Encountering his patients' resistance to recalling certain memories, Freud writes:

> The same forces which, in the form of resistance, were now offering opposition to the forgotten material's being made conscious, must formerly have brought about the forgetting and must have pushed the pathogenic experiences in question out of consciousness. I gave the name of 'repression' to this pathological process, and I considered that it was proved by the undeniable existence of resistance.
>
> *(Freud 1910: 19–20)*

Bollas states that 'an individual preconsciously represses unwanted feelings, ideas and experiences to the unconscious, where such banished contents immediately constitute a nucleus of interlocking ideas' (Bollas 1992b: 72). Each nucleus of repressed material, unable to return to consciousness, collects further ideas and affects which are repressed in their turn. Bollas argues that this pathological process, which increasingly diminishes the person's self-awareness, is not the only route by which material passes into the unconscious. He writes that 'to complement the theory of repression, we need a *theory of reception* which designates some ideas as the received rather than the repressed', and that the aim of this reception is 'to allow unconscious development without the intrusive effect of consciousness' (ibid.: 74). Unlike repression, which banishes certain threatening ideas from consciousness, reception allows material that is potentially life-enhancing to be stored and developed out of awareness:

> the ego understands that unconscious work is necessary to develop a part of the personality, to elaborate a phantasy, to allow for the evolution of a nascent emotional experience, and ideas or feelings and words are sent to the system unconscious, not to be banished but to be given a mental space for development which is not possible in consciousness.
>
> *(Bollas 1992b: 74)*

The receptive unconscious can be seen as the unconscious counterpart of Mills' mental shed, an internal studio into which potentially useful elements are invited and within which they are stored until some connection between them emerges.

From the concept of the receptive unconscious, Bollas goes on to develop his theory of psychic genera. He suggests that when lived experience evokes intense interest, an inner space is created within which a generative psychic structure begins to form. The initial area of interest constitutes a 'psychic gravity' which attracts related elements (feelings, perceptions, ideas) and, unconsciously, new links are formed. He postulates a series of steps in the formation of genera: 1. There is a moment when lived experience evokes intense psychic interest and evoked feelings, ideas and self-states come together and create an unconscious desire for their development. This results in the 'conception' of an inner space devoted to the formation of a 'generative psychic structure'. 2. This results in a 'psychic gravity' that attracts relevant data. 3. The unconscious collection of links to the psychic complex results in a sense of chaos which must be tolerated and facilitated. 4. Gradually, a sense of cohesion or 'nucleation' begins to form. 5. The new idea emerges. Bollas writes that the moment when an idea emerges may feel revelatory (as the artists' quotations in the next chapter, 'Illumination and the idea', show), and he writes 'although it is a special experience it is not an occasion for a new theory of the sacred, but it does describe those seminal visions created by unconscious processes pushed by the life instincts' (ibid.: 89).

Bollas' model depends on the concept that 'relevant data' are actively stored in the receptive unconscious. For the visual artist, the data would relate to the elements that will eventually be integrated in the idea for the new work: elements from the outside world of shared experience, elements from the artist's own internal experience, and visual considerations. I am suggesting here that the collection of these data is, in Bollas' terms, 'pushed by the life instincts' (this assumes that the artist is not working with traumatic material from the repressed unconscious. Works of art may also be created from a position of trauma, but it is beyond the scope of this book to explore this trajectory in detail.) The receptive unconscious provides a space protected from the artist's own potential judgement, within which links between these areas can be formed.

Bollas does not give a full explanation of the way in which the sense of cohesion or nucleation of stage 4 occurs. Writing 25 years earlier, the educationalist Anton Ehrenzweig, considering the work of artists, formulated the idea of an unconscious 'womb' which seems to have something in common with Bollas' concept of the 'receptive unconscious'. Within this 'womb', there are 'fruitful dedifferentiations' and the integration of different elements can occur through the 'unlimited mutual interpenetration of oceanic imagery' (Ehrenzweig 1967: 192). Here, Ehrenzweig is writing about a process that goes on in parallel with the artist's work with her medium rather than the earlier phase before the emergence of an idea, but his concept of dedifferentiation helps to shed light on the way in which cohesion between different elements in the receptive unconscious may occur. Ehrenzweig's 'undifferentiated matrix' is dominated by the primary process and by equivalence rather than discrimination. Dedifferentiation allows elements that seem disparate to the conscious mind to link together through unexpected concordances.

Bollas also does not explain why the new idea emerges into consciousness at a particular point, except to say that a sense of cohesion precedes this emergence. For the artist, following the theory of the artist's process that I develop in this book, I propose that this happens if and when the process of linking different elements in the receptive unconscious (following Ehrenzweig, this would be through dedifferentiation) results in an image or idea that resonates very closely with the unformed inner experience touched on in the pre-sense. When this occurs, the artist's sense of 'fit' between idea and pre-sense is sufficiently strong to breach the barrier that keeps this inner work out of the artist's awareness and the idea irrupts suddenly into consciousness.

Bollas' stages of psychic genera can be related to the sub-stages of the artist's process that I discuss in the first three chapters of this book. The stage when 'lived experience evokes intense psychic interest' relates to the sub-stage of 'the pre-sense' discussed in Chapter 1, and can be equated with the moment when something in the outside world resonates with something internal for the artist and gives rise to the desire, or the compulsion, to make a new work. The 'psychic gravity' that attracts relevant data relates to the stage of preparation and research discussed in this chapter. Bollas' stage of unconscious linking would correspond to the stage of gestation, also discussed in this chapter, and the new idea, which Bollas describes as 'a fundamentally new perspective', is discussed in Chapter 3.

The division of the process of creative problem-solving into stages has a number of precedents, particularly in the work of social psychologist Graham Wallas (1926) and later writers who have developed his ideas. Drawing on the introspective reports of thinkers such as the mathematician and physicist Henri Poincaré and the physicist Hermann von Helmholtz, Wallas proposed one of the first models of the creative process. He postulated four stages of creative thinking. The first stage is 'preparation', in which the creative person immerses him- or herself in the problem and consciously attempts to solve it. If no solution is found, the person puts the problem aside. The second phase is 'incubation' when, according to Wallas, there is an unconscious sifting and sorting of the material amassed earlier and new associations or combinations are tried out. If these unconscious processes result in a new and relevant linking, then this leads to a third stage, 'illumination', at which point the new idea comes into consciousness. This may be preceded by a sense, on the 'fringe' of consciousness, that an idea is imminent. Wallas calls this 'intimation'. Finally, the idea is tested consciously in the phase of 'verification'.

Wallas' stages partially map onto the stages of the artist's process I describe, but there are differences. Wallas is concerned with problem-solving, and he assumes that a problem has already been identified. For many artists, there is an earlier stage that I have called the pre-sense, and the 'problem' of the work is initiated by the pre-sense. Hayley Newman says:

> the hunch is . . . for me, more of an indication. I mean the hunch itself creates the problem, in a way. Because, I follow the hunch and then I have to . . . make sense of the problems that arise out of the hunch.
>
> (Newman 2011)

A further, very important, difference between Wallas' model and the artist's process is that Wallas assumes there is a right answer to the problem and that this can be verified in the final stage. This may apply to creative processes in the sciences, but it is not relevant to the artist. For the artist, the idea is, in many ways, just the beginning of the work, as I will discuss in later chapters of this book.

3

ILLUMINATION AND THE IDEA

It's about recognising something when it's coming towards the surface where you can catch it.
Liz Rideal

Philosopher Michael Polanyi, in his book *Personal Knowledge*, describes four phases of discovery, writing: 'true discovery is not strictly logical performance, and accordingly, we may describe the obstacle to be overcome in solving a problem as the 'logical gap' . . . 'Illumination' is then the leap by which the logical gap is crossed' (Polanyi 1962: 123). Polanyi is writing about discovery, not the artist's process, but his evocative metaphor of a leap across a gap speaks to the experience of the sudden arrival of an idea. A 'leap' is necessary to arrive at 'illumination', or the new idea.

In this chapter, I want to think about what it feels like to have an idea and the conditions in which ideas might emerge. I will start with my own experience of the emergence of an idea for a new piece in the Morecambe Bay series:

> *For a long time, I felt that nothing was happening. My playing around with different approaches did not satisfy me and I was not clear about exactly what I wanted to do. Then, suddenly, the idea came to me that I wanted to bring the sands to life and an image of how I might do that came into my mind. I would take still photographs of the channels of water in the sands, returning to the same spot on consecutive days. I would then create an animation of these photographs. I felt that the animation would enliven the still images and convey the idea of a movement over time. It would, I hoped, also capture something of the sense of instability, danger and the threat of being overwhelmed that the sands evoked in me.*

The visual image that came to mind was both a reflection of my inner experience and a transformed view of the outer world of the sands. It 'looked right' to me.

This looking right included a sense that the form embodied not only those aspects of my experience of which I was aware but also something that I could not yet define.

Many artists described the experience of the sudden and unexpected irruption of an idea in dramatic terms: 'It did come in a flash' (Jo Volley) or it was 'a leap of inspiration' (David Johnson) or 'Actually I had a complete epiphany, a sort of frisson' (Liz Rideal). These descriptions imply a discontinuity between the conscious thoughts that were going on before this moment and the idea itself. This is the logical gap described by Polanyi. The 'inspired' idea has not come through logical reasoning but by a 'leap' to something new. For some, this occurred only rarely and, when it did, it signalled the beginning of a new series of works. For others, each new work was heralded by the spark of an unexpected idea. These experiences were clearly differentiated from the more gradual development of an idea through research or through working with a medium (although new ideas or new directions for an ongoing idea might also arise during work with the medium). Simon Faithfull describes the way in which such an idea came to him during a meeting with a curator:

> It was this sort of vision of, in a way, leaving myself behind and what that would be. It would be a camera attached to a weather balloon that I would sort of let go of, and it would be an eye looking back at myself, getting smaller, smaller and smaller. Almost like an out of body experience. That's what I wanted it to be like. . . . As far as I can tell I came up with that in that moment which really amazes me. It must have been knocking around – I have done other things with balloons – but I'd never actually crystallised it, or it'd never come out of solution, so to speak, until that moment when I absolutely needed to have an idea . . . Something about what happened revealed to me something about the nature of those ideas: that they're in solution and then at some moment drop out of solution and sort of become crystallised. They feel like there's something I've been chewing on and mulling over but in a very unstructured incoherent way.
>
> (Faithfull 2012)

Faithfull's idea came to him as a 'vision', an image of what the final piece might look like. In using the metaphor of crystallisation, he seems to suggest that something was waiting 'in solution' in the unconscious until a particular circumstance (in this case, the meeting) acted as a catalyst for it to assume a particular shape and irrupt into consciousness. Pursuing the chemical analogy, the interaction and combination of different elements in the unconscious might be compared to a chemical reaction. Faithfull says, 'I've done other things with balloons'. He has also done other things with film. So this idea brings together aspects of earlier works, of elements in the outside world (including balloons, cameras, reports of out-of-body experiences) and of elements from the artist's own internal experience.

Occasionally, a period of gestation may be followed not by the advent of a new idea but by the discovery of something in the outside world that seems to correspond almost perfectly with something inner. More usually, the artist needs to abstract those elements of the outer something that are essential to her experience. But sometimes, it seems that no abstraction is necessary. I describe my own experience of such a moment:

> *One evening I went to a stretch of the shore that I often visited. I was intending to take some still photographs in the evening light. On this occasion, as on many others, I was aware that I was searching for something, though I had only a vague idea of what it was I hoped to find. On my solitary trips to the Bay I felt myself to be in a particular state of mind. It was as if I was in a bubble of time, a space of my own, in which I could detach myself from the concerns of everyday life. I was in a state in which I was highly tuned to elements in the landscape that seemed to resonate with something in me. On this particular evening I found something unexpected. A small spring of water emerged from underneath the sands, danced before my eyes, reflecting the setting sun, and then disappeared beneath the ground again, only to re-emerge moments later. I was immediately captivated by the sight as if it was exactly this phenomenon that I had been waiting for without knowing it. All I had to do, it seemed, was to capture it on film. Of course, having made my film, there followed a process of revision and editing to produce the final work. But, in this case, whatever doubts I had about the details of the final presentation, I knew that the film reflected something of the sense of danger and instability and the threat of being overwhelmed that I was trying to reach.*
>
> *(see Figure 3.1)*

On this occasion, I already knew that I wanted to make a work related to Morecambe Bay. I was looking for something, although I did not know what that something was. I had already been through a period of preparation and experimentation and a period of waiting (gestation). When I discovered the spring, I seemed to *recognise* it as if I had been searching for just this phenomenon. By using the word 'recognition', I do not intend to imply a conscious cognitive process. Rather, the experience was an emotional one of sensing a 'fit' between the spring and something internal. Also, the spring not only 'felt right' but it also 'looked right': in that moment of seeing the spring, I could visualise the potential work within the trajectory of my own artistic practice. Although I had only a still camera with me, I knew that a still image would not do. The movement was essential. I must take the risk of leaving the spring in order to fetch a video camera, knowing that the particular effect that had captivated me might not last until I returned. My sense of what 'looked right' was coloured by my knowledge of the history of gallery film and of contemporary video artworks. It was also influenced by artworks in many media that related to circles (including those by Richard Long, Wassily Kandinsky and Damien Hirst). I had myself

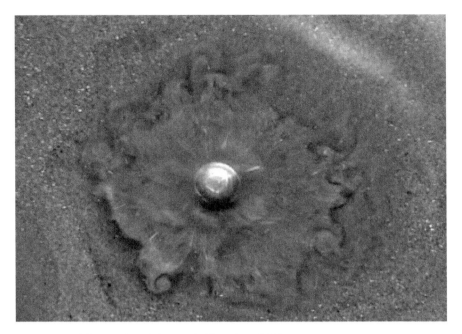

FIGURE 3.1 *The Quick and the Dead.* SD video, 2009

made previous photographic and installation works related to stone circles (*The Circles They Desire* and *Witches' Dance*). In particular, this new work was closely related to an earlier piece, *Full Circle*, a looped film in which water drains and refills from a plughole. The new work, *The Quick and the Dead*, re-engaged with the concerns of the previous film, particularly the terror of annihilation, figured in the earlier work by water spiralling and disappearing down a drain. *The Quick and the Dead* renders the form of the feared annihilation more specific by involving a different aspect of the outside world, the landscape of Morecambe Bay. Here, water is sucked into the body of the sands.

It is likely that my memory of *Full Circle*, though out of my awareness at the time, contributed to my sense of recognition when I came across the spring. This experience is a rare occurrence for me, and in making other works the process is much more tortuous. When no ready-made form is to be found, I must wait for an idea about how I might construct one for myself.

Sometimes gestation leading to a new idea can occur during sleep. Judith Goddard described a dream that presented a clear image of an animated film that she then went on to create. Although her experience of a mental picture of a complete work has not been repeated, this artist still finds that ideas come to her as she wakes:

When I wake up in the morning the first thoughts I have are probably the most important. That's a treasured time for me, that waking time and the best ideas for me come just when I'm first awake . . . these ideas for work just burst out first thing in the morning and that's rather wonderful.

(Goddard 2011)

Goddard's sense of wonder at a new idea was also described by other artists who spoke of feelings of 'excitement' or elation, a heightened state of mind. Sharon Kivland describes her experience:

It's almost like an image flash of something that I want to see. Now I don't know what it is but then I go about trying to find it . . . it's a fairly abstract vision and . . . in the fantasy of it I don't have to enter into the difficulties of production . . . [it's] unframed by anything that would undo its wonder, its miraculous quality.

(Kivland 2011)

In that moment, for this artist, the new idea seems perfect, even miraculous. Kivland senses something 'marvellous', and its 'wonder' is linked with the fact that it is 'unframed'. It is not fully defined, and this lack of clear delineation allows the artist to sense the idea or image as unlimited, as more than just itself. This is the case even though the artist knows from experience that this heightened state of mind will not last for long.

When I began my research, this was one of the elements of my own experience that I hoped to clarify. In a similar way to Kivland, I felt entranced by new ideas:

It is exciting. I feel elated. The idea feels brilliant, as if it is perfect. Whilst these ideas are still in my mind and have not yet been realised in the outside world they remain full of potential. They are not yet clearly defined. If they do not feel quite right they can be instantly changed in my imagination. In this state of mind, internal judgemental voices are silenced.

Through my interviews, I found that many other artists experience similar feelings when a new idea arises. The image of a potential new work often seems to be both new and familiar. One interviewee says: 'It's a little flash of inspiration but maybe not inspiration but recognition' (John Aiken). This corresponds with my own experience in that, when an idea arises, I do feel that it is somehow familiar even though it is new to me.

Bollas argues that one of the functions of the receptive unconscious is to provide a space in which the developing ideas are safe from the judgements of consciousness. I extend this to suggest that, at the moment of the emergence of the idea, and for a short time thereafter, these judgements remain suspended. But I think that there is more to this state of mind than suspension of criticism. I think that the sense of recognition and the elation stem from the initial belief that there is a perfect 'fit' between the idea and the inner experience. At the moment of its emergence, the idea is still 'an abstract vision', closely connected to the pre-sense and to all the elements that were linked to it in the receptive unconscious. Only later will it be seen in a more realistic way, and at that point it is likely to fall from grace.

In order to dig a little deeper into the question of why the new idea is idealised, I want to turn to the work of psychiatrist and psychoanalyst Ignacio Matte Blanco (1980) on the functioning of the unconscious. Matte Blanco reasons that, although unconscious thought does not follow the rules of conscious logic, it must have a logic of its own. In order to make sense of the world around us, we constantly classify objects, comparing them to other objects with which we are familiar. Matte Blanco points out that this requires both a recognition of similarities (in order to categorise objects) and the discrimination of differences. He argues that this involves an interweaving of two types of logical thought: 'asymmetric' logic, the logic of discrimination whereby differences are recognised, and 'symmetric logic', the logic of sameness, whereby opposites are treated as identical and parts of objects are treated as equivalent to the whole. Matte Blanco shows how the processes of the unconscious discovered by Freud, such as condensation, displacement and timelessness, can be understood in terms of symmetric logic.

It is beyond the scope of this book to follow Matte Blanco's full argument, but I want to indicate how he brings in the concept of infinity through his use of mathematical set theory. A set is simply a collection of items that have something in common and, according to mathematical set theory, a subset is equivalent to a whole set only when the set is infinite. For a non-mathematician, this may seem difficult to comprehend, but the psychoanalyst Eric Rayner (1981) gives an example to illustrate the point: a sequence of numbers from 1 to infinity is an infinite set. But so is the subset of even numbers. That is, there are as many even numbers as whole numbers (i.e. infinity), despite the fact that the original set also includes odd numbers. Martin Creed offers a non-mathematical example of the same point in his *Work No. 232. The whole world + the work = the whole world* (2000). The concept of a subset being equated with a whole infinite set is linked to the fact that, according to symmetric logic, parts can be felt to be equivalent to the whole and can be felt to possess a quality of infinity. I think that this is relevant to the artist's initial idealisation of a new idea. The partial fit between idea and inner experience is experienced as total, and the idea seems to be infinitely wonderful. Discussing the work of Matte Blanco, Rayner describes the way in which this symmetrisation operates when someone falls in love:

> At its height . . . infinites hold sway, parts tend to be identical to wholes, time and space stand still. Idealization with its sense of infinity dominates . . . These extreme emotional states display qualities of irradiation and maximization. Also, time and space tend to disappear.
>
> *(Rayner 1981: 58)*

Rayner's description could apply equally to the feeling of the artist towards the new idea (although the artist's feeling is likely to be considerably more fleeting than that of the person in love). That is, at the moment of the idea's emergence, unconscious symmetric logic still holds sway so that the idea seems to be perfectly attuned to her inner experience and to have infinite possibilities. Only later, when the rules of asymmetric logic regain their place in conscious thought, will this feeling fade and discrepancies emerge. I return to this in Chapter 4.

The artists' descriptions suggest that certain conditions are necessary to enable the new idea to emerge. Many interviewees made the point that unexpected ideas tend not to arise when they are actively working on a problem. Rather, the flash of insight occurs when they are in a relaxed state or their mind is occupied with something else:

> *The pieces that I'm most proud of, most happy with, generally come into my imagination fully formed in like eureka moments when I'm in the bath or in bed or having a walk – not normally when I'm making art. But obviously they don't come from nowhere. They come when I've been thinking really hard about something for a long time or I've been reading something new . . . It will be in a moment of calm and I'm not concentrating on any of that I guess everything congeals into an idea.*
>
> *(Lovett 2011)*

It seems that a state of relaxation, following an extended period of preparation, provides the conditions in which a new idea can emerge (although it is not clear whether the idea has been formed earlier but can only emerge in these conditions or whether the crucial links between elements in the receptive unconscious are made at the moment the idea makes itself known).

But this is not the only state of mind in which ideas might arise. When Simon Faithfull's idea arose in the context of a meeting with a curator, quoted earlier, he can hardly be said to have been relaxed. He describes the context in detail:

> *I went to have a meeting with a curator, and I showed him some past work, and everybody liked it, and then there was obviously a moment for me to say what I would like to maybe develop, and I had one thing up my sleeve. The curator had really liked the piece of finished work that I showed him, then I said this new idea but it wasn't right for him . . . It was actually a bit of a break for me then, having this meeting with this curator. So, it was a lot of pressure. I was like ' . . . I haven't got anything to show, or to tempt him with. I need to come up with something, but right now.' That's what I felt in that moment, and, sort of – in that moment – came up with this idea which would then become this quite big commission for me. [. . .] Half of the time my best ideas happen when I'm asleep, that's not exactly true, but I think it is when they kind of catch me off guard in a sort of a non-structured state . . . Or in extremes, like in those situations. Probably that situation with the curator is more unusual, but still – even in that situation – it was like 'where the xxxx did that come from?' But I needed it, and it was obviously somewhere waiting to come out of solution.*
>
> *(Faithfull 2012)*

So, for Faithfull, there seem to be two possible states of mind in which ideas might emerge. One is when he is in a 'non-structured state' that he links with sleep. This suggests that it might be a semi-conscious state, such as that experienced on first waking. The other situation is 'in extremes', when under pressure. At first sight, it may seem that there is little in common between these two situations. But a link may be discerned if we see them both as times when the artist's attention is withdrawn from a conscious consideration of a problem. In the situation of the meeting with the curator, Faithfull's attention had been focused on the idea he had prepared. When this was rejected, he suddenly had nothing to focus on at a conscious level. It was at this point that the new idea sprang to mind.

Returning to Bollas, and his description of the receptive unconscious and psychic genera, he writes that the withdrawal of conscious focusing allows a lifting of 'the protective barrier provided by the anti-cathexes[1] of pre-consciousness' (Bollas 1992b: 73). Then, provided that the unconscious work of psychic genera has progressed to the point where an idea has been formed, this idea or image is able to emerge from the receptive unconscious into consciousness. Here, Bollas is referring to Freud's topographical model of the mind in which Freud differentiates between the system unconscious, the system conscious and the pre-conscious. The contents of the preconscious are out of awareness but are, in principle, accessible to consciousness. In Bollas' terms, the 'anticathexes of pre-consciousness' act as a barrier to prevent unconscious contents from reaching consciousness. He suggests that 'conscious focusing' has the effect of keeping this barrier in place, whereas the relaxation of this focus allows a more fluid movement between unconscious, preconscious and conscious. However, not all unconscious contents are capable of reaching consciousness. Bollas is specifically referring to the contents of the receptive unconscious and, staying with the topographical model, I understand him to mean that the formation of an idea through the work of psychic genera leads to its availability to the pre-conscious and hence to consciousness. Applying this to the theory I develop in this chapter, when the work of linking taking place out of the artist's awareness results in an idea or image that is very close to the unformed inner experience touched on in the 'pre-sense', the artist's recognition of this fit is sufficiently strong to bring it to consciousness at a moment when the withdrawal of conscious focusing has attenuated the anti-cathexes of pre-consciousness.

In the previous pages, I have traced the trajectory towards an idea for a new work. But not all artists begin a new work with a single idea. For some, there is a more gradual development through an experimental engagement with their medium. The initial exploratory engagement with the medium, described in the previous chapter, might flow without any clear division of stages into the development of the artwork I describe in the next chapter.

The sculptor Phyllida Barlow wants the behaviour of her materials to disclose what it is she wishes to explore:

> *I'm interested in the act itself – whether it's pulled, stretched . . . I want the actions to lead me to the image. I don't have a subject. I hope the subject will reveal itself*

*through the process . . . I am interested in whether the process has engaged me –
whether I'm surprised or alarmed – that is a signal that it is has some sort of life
about it.*

(Barlow 2012)

Here, it seems that the trajectory towards an idea that I have discussed in this
chapter is turned on its head. Barlow's ideas come later, arising out of her work
with her medium. Her emotional response to her process is her guide as to
whether she is on a promising track or not.

Whereas Barlow says she wants the 'subject' to emerge as she works with the
medium, O'Donoghue says that he has a 'subject' when he begins a painting but
his 'ideas' cannot be considered as separate from the work with his medium.
These 'ideas' or visualisations may emerge both from research and through the
act of painting itself:

*I think that really the practice of painting, the idea isn't something separate, it's inte-
gral to my activity as a painter . . . it's how the idea is given form that makes an idea
interesting . . . I would liken my process to an archaeologist digging for something.
When I'm making a painting it's a bit like that. I'm excavating a subject and so certain things may be in that that I'm not really consciously aware of. And that happens
frequently in a work, and that's usually the thing that's most interesting, is the thing
that's dredged up from . . . the subconscious because then it's usually quite profound,
and it's not literal . . . ideas are sort of constantly there and I may, you know, stop
painting and come in here and look something up in a book that's occurred to me, or
read something or go to a particular reference and I think this bringing together, this
connecting of things, is what's very, very exciting for me in art, where you get these
kind of subliminal connections.*

(O'Donoghue 2013)

Barlow and O'Donoghue use the word 'subject' in different ways in the above
quotations. For O'Donoghue, his 'subject' corresponds to the finding of an area
of interest, whereas Barlow uses the term to denote something more like an 'idea'
(as I define it). O'Donoghue's use of the word 'idea' does not only denote a first
image of a possible work, as I have used it in this chapter. He is also referring to
ongoing ideas for shifts in direction or modifications of the original idea arising
out of the work itself. It seems that, in his process, research and experimentation,
which I have designated as a stage leading to the idea, is intimately tied in with
the making process itself (which I explore in the next chapter). This demonstrates
the fact that the artist's process is not linear and that the phases I outline in this
book may overlap or be repeated at any stage.

O'Donoghue acknowledges the unconscious work that results in exciting
connections. This is the realm of the receptive unconscious where the bringing
together of disparate elements can take place. The analogy that O'Donoghue
draws between his process and that of the archaeologist brings to mind the fact

that Freud used the same metaphor to describe the work of psychoanalysis (Freud 1937: 259–260). O'Donoghue's 'dredging up from the subconscious' is a phrase that could equally be used of the psychoanalytic process. The use of the word 'dredging' adds a further dimension to the archaeological digging, suggesting that what is being brought to the surface has been submerged in the waters of the unconscious. Both the artist and the patient bring unconscious contents into relation with consciousness and the world of shared reality. However, the artist must go a step further: the bringing together of inner and outer must be achieved within a form that satisfies her as an art object.

Note

1 Freud uses this term for the defensive activity of the ego in impeding the access to consciousness of unconscious desires and wishes (Freud 1916–1917: 438).

4

WORKING WITH THE MEDIUM

What you've got is something that's got its own life, its own energy and therefore you auto-matically are in a dialogue with it because it's different.

John Aiken

In the previous chapter, I described the way in which an idea for a new work arises and the sense of elation that the artist may feel. Now I want to consider what happens next. There is a time gap, sometimes very short and sometimes more protracted, between the arrival of the idea and the beginning of the artist's work with her medium. One interviewee, Eleanor Morgan, describes this point as 'joyfully secret and privileged – to have this moment when something only exists in your head'. Initially, the new idea may be a private pleasure. Indeed, I have found from my own experience that talking about an idea too early can stop me in my tracks. I have learned that, at this early stage, I need to protect the idea not only from my own possible judgements but also from those of other people. On the other hand, for artists who work collaboratively, sharing ideas may be a central part of their process. As Thomson and Craighead say: 'The discussion becomes the place where the idea grows.'

But whether or not they share their ideas, many of the interviewees described a sense of disappointment when they begin to work with their medium. At this point, the idea often seems to lose its aura of perfection. Gina Glover, a photographer, says: 'I have the film processed and I just look at them and they are often quite disappointing . . . it's generally always disappointing. I've learned not to worry.' Through long experience, this artist has learned that disappointment is an *inevitable* part of her process. Here, I want to think about this experience of disappointment or disillusionment and the reasons why it might occur.

Simon Faithfull describes how he deals with the 'gap' between his idea and its actualisation:

> *Almost every work has that gap and some of them never make it out of that gap. But the successful ones there's always a process of disappointment and then scrabbling back up and making it work, connecting with the initial excitement in fulfilling what you thought you had nailed down which actually turned out not to be.*
>
> *(Faithfull 2012)*

Faithfull speaks of 'nailing down' his idea, a metaphor that alludes to the physicality of this new phase of working with the medium. The idea is elusive, resisting clear definition, so that no physical manifestation can completely capture it. There is always something lacking, a sense of loss and disenchantment. But Faithfull might be able to retrieve something valuable. His description of 'scrabbling back up' suggests a process involving effort and engagement with setbacks as he tries to find a form for his experience that is robust enough to exist as an object in the outside world whilst also regaining some of the 'initial excitement' of the idea.

For established artists such as the interviewees, this experience of disenchantment is no surprise. They have learned to expect and accept it, but they may nevertheless regret the passing of the euphoria of the initial idea. Another interviewee delays beginning work with her medium so that she can continue to enjoy her elated state of mind for a little longer:

> *I'm putting it off, I'm putting it off in case it's terrible. In case it's weak. There's that moment . . . before one has the terrible realisation of its . . . inherent badness . . . or before one has to open oneself up to failure.*
>
> *(Kivland 2011)*

I do not think that this potential 'failure' or weakness is primarily the possible negative judgement of an audience. Rather, it seems to be linked to the artist's own disappointment once she begins to work with her medium. I think that the 'inherent badness' that this artist refers to is due to the inevitable gap between the inner idea, still replete with all its unconscious associations, and its more limited external form. As long as the idea has not been given an external form, it is almost infinitely plastic as if anything is possible. Once the artist starts work with her medium, choices have to be made and each choice excludes others.

In the previous chapter, I proposed that the artist's elation when a new idea emerges is due to a sense of a perfect fit between the idea and the inner experience that gave rise to it. Initially, the idea is closely connected to the pre-sense and to all the elements that were linked to it in the receptive unconscious. It still trails the trappings of infinity, of unboundedness. The artist feels as if anything is possible. At this stage, she may experience a sense of 'at-oneness' with her own seemingly perfect idea. But as soon as she starts to engage with the medium, the idea begins to be framed, defined and 'nailed down', and this process inevitably excludes the more elusive aspects of the unbounded idea. At this point, the artist is confronted by the limits intrinsic to her chosen medium. Paint behaves in a certain way, the camera produces certain types of images, certain manipulations are possible using a computer program and so on. It is no longer the case that anything is possible.

However, the interviewees have learned from experience that if they let go of the seemingly ideal image/idea, then they can begin to make use of the medium, interacting with it and responding to its properties. Gina Glover says she has 'learned not to worry' because she knows that she will move on to work with her medium to develop the work in ways she had not foreseen. As she says: 'I know what I'm looking for but I know it's going to shift.' The interviewees have come to recognise and respect the particular qualities of their various media and welcome their otherness as providing them with the means to take their work forward. The way is opened for an interaction between artist and medium in which each can be pliable in response to the other.

For the artist who has a preliminary idea, the next stage is to use her medium to find a material form for this idea or image. One interviewee says:

> The process of making it is mostly a matter of trying to translate the visual thing I have in my mind – the experiential feeling about it I have in my mind, into the finished object. If there's any translation at all involved it is usually some mechanical thing that didn't work quite how I expected.
>
> (Johnson 2011)

The 'visual thing' that Johnson has in mind is what I am calling his idea and 'the experiential feeling' is his sense of the interaction between inner and outer worlds that gave rise to his 'pre-sense'. The 'experiential feeling' is haptic or visceral and is not clearly defined, whilst the 'visual thing' is a more specific image of the possible form of the new work. This particular artist sees the development of his idea, before he starts work with his medium, as the most important part of his process. He is unusual among the interviewees in saying that 'In many ways making work is usually quite mechanical' and claiming that the final work does not usually differ greatly from the idea. However, he does say that the medium may do something unexpected that could sometimes call for an adaptation of the idea.

Most of the interviewees lay much greater emphasis than Johnson on the making stage of their process and on the behaviour of their medium. The medium responds to the artist's actions in particular ways, depending on its own properties, and frequently the developing artwork does not go according to plan. As the painter Jo Volley describes her process:

> You've got an idea and you want to do it and you think you've got the best way of doing it but of course when you've done it it's actually not what I wanted. So it can be 'That's not what I wanted but it's actually quite interesting' or 'How do I get it how I wanted?' but you have to do it a different way, not the way you thought it would be at all.
>
> (Volley 2011)

This artist describes two different possible reactions to the discovery that the medium is not giving her the effect she intended. The medium does something else, something unexpected, and the artist may reject this unexpected effect and try to find an alternative use of her medium to pursue her original direction. On the other hand, this surprising effect may turn out to be a revelation, resulting in the discovery of an exciting new way of realising her project. If there was an initial idea, this might be modified (without losing the connection with the guiding pre-sense).

Dana Schutz, a painter, describes the way in which her paint resists her intentions:

> You know what you want it to be like and then it goes off the rails . . . the paint will do its own thing. It is a physical dance, you respond to it and if it is going well you forget that you are painting, it just feels like you are responding to it.
>
> *(Schutz 2013: 59)*

Schutz has an idea or mental image of what she wants, but the paint itself takes her in an unforeseen direction. A complex interaction is set in motion in which artist and medium respond to each other in a smooth and spontaneous way. But is this dance-like movement peculiar to the interaction of painter and paint, or does it apply to the use of other media? One of the interviewees, Dryden Goodwin, describes his interaction with his camera:

> *There's something about the positive feedback you get from putting a pencil on a page. For me that relates to how I want to use the camera. And you know, I suppose there is a kind of relationship between the sort of touching with the eye or touching with the lens . . . there's a nervousness . . . will you be able to find a way of holding that within the limitations of what the camera can do? But then pushing what the camera can do.*
>
> *(Goodwin 2011)*

As in the case of Schutz, there is a mutually responsive interaction between artist and medium. For Goodwin, it is as if artist and camera are working together, testing each other's capacities and limitations. Goodwin's comparison between the physical contact of pencil and paper and the visual contact of looking (either directly or through the camera lens) seems to speak to the sense of a close connection between the artist and his subject. His nervousness is related to the question of whether he will be able to push both his own actions and the capabilities of his camera to accommodate what he wants to express about this connection.

These artists describe the way in which they use their chosen medium to externalise their inner experience. They are dependent on the medium (already in the external world) to help them to do this. But their descriptions show that the medium is not merely a passive tool. Rather, its responses can radically affect the course of the work. Goodwin needs his camera both to have its own characteristics that will direct his work and to be flexible enough to bend to his purpose. In a sense, the artist enters into a collaboration or partnership with the medium to achieve her ends.

I want to explore the nature of the collaboration between artist and medium by bringing in the work of two psychoanalysts who have drawn on the work of Donald Winnicott. Ken Wright refers to Winnicott's concept of mirroring (Winnicott 1986a), together with Daniel Stern's work on maternal attunement (Stern 1985), to draw a parallel between the relationship between mother and child and the artist's relationship with her medium (Wright 2009a). Winnicott writes that, in the course of healthy development, the mother mirrors the infant in the sense that her loving gaze allows the baby to see himself reflected in his mother's face: 'The mother is looking at the baby and *what she looks like is related to what she sees there*' (Winnicott 1986a: 131). This mirroring can be seen as an aspect of the adaptive mother in that the mother's face reflects her response to the infant's internal state just as the 'breast' corresponds with the infant's need and anticipation. Daniel Stern's work on attunement extends the concept of mirroring to include the ways in which a mother responds to her baby's feeling states not only through her facial expression but also by her movements and her voice. If the mother is attuned to her baby, she is engaged in a constantly changing interaction in which her bodily gestures, facial expressions and utterances all reflect the baby's state of mind. This reflection provides the infant with forms for his unformed experiences and the baby begins to constitute a sense of himself from the forms that he receives from his mother or caregiver: 'in the mother–infant relationship, maternal forms reveal the essence of the infant's experience to him, and provide him with a means of experiencing himself' (Wright 2014).

Wright argues that these attuned forms 'constitute the containers of vital experience on which the integrity of the self depends', and he contends that the developing artwork can fulfil a similar function for the artist. According to Wright, the artist is engaged in a struggle with her medium in which she attempts to mould it into a form that is attuned to her inner experience, a form that can act as a mirror for her. However, unlike the baby, whose good-enough mother spontaneously provides mirroring and adaptive forms, the artist must herself act on the medium to make it perform these functions 'as though the creative person, in the act of creation, performs for himself the activities which the adaptive mother once provided' (Wright 2009b: 62).

The work of René Roussillon is also informed by Winnicott's work on the early relationship between mother and infant and the need for the mother to be responsive to her baby's signals. Roussillon, a French psychoanalyst who integrates Freudian theory and the French psychoanalytic tradition with Winnicott's thinking, takes up Marion Milner's concept of the 'pliable medium' when discussing the infant's need for his mother to be flexible enough to respond to his needs. Considering the early mother–child relationship and referring to Milner's work, he writes:

> Milner emphasises the fundamental part played . . . by an encounter with an object that is a sufficiently pliable medium: in other words, with an object that can let itself be transformed in accordance with the requirements of the infant's creative process. It is thanks to that good enough malleability that the mothering environment can fulfil its role as 'mirror': by making itself malleable so as to respond to the internal states and impulses, it can make adjustments to the reflection that give substance to that narcissistic function.
>
> *(Roussillon 2015a: 100)*

Roussillon, like Wright, compares the malleability of the mother to that of the artist's medium which must be responsive enough to the artist's actions. But Roussillon returns to this subject, recognising that both infant and artist encounter a medium that is not only pliable but also resistant:

> The subject's effort to 'become subject' will thus be an effort 'at all costs' to render this rigid environment 'malleable'. This is what, for example, the work of sculpture makes clear: starting with a hard material and transforming it until it may accommodate a representation . . . In any creative work we must be able to identify this process at work; perhaps it even signals that which characterizes creative work, which always, when substantial, meets with a form of resistance of the material to be transformed.
>
> *(Roussillon 2015b: 593)*

Roussillon cites sculpture in which the medium itself is made malleable and transformed into the developing artwork. This is not the case for all artforms. For instance, Goodwin's camera (discussed above) is not a material in this way, but nevertheless it acts as a medium that both resists his actions (through the limitations of its capabilities) and can be made malleable (by responding to his actions and, perhaps, going beyond its normal possibilities). The correspondence between the malleability of the mothering environment and that of the artist's medium proposed by Roussillon is clear, but the maternal equivalent of the medium's 'resistance' seems to me to be more complex. The artist encounters a resistant medium that has to be made malleable by her own efforts. There is a movement from resistance to malleability. For the baby, the 'resistance' of the mother-medium lies in the fact that the mother is a person in her own right with her own needs that may not coincide with those of her baby. At first, the infant (not yet a 'subject' in his own right) treats her as a part of himself and, if all goes well, she adapts more or less fully to this demand. Winnicott calls this state 'primary maternal preoccupation' (Winnicott 1975). Later, she begins to assert her own needs again. Winnicott describes the process by which the baby is gradually disillusioned as the mother does not attune herself perfectly to his needs. The baby learns that he does not have complete control over his mother and, if the disillusionment is manageable, he begins to make his own adaptations to what is available (I am assuming that the mother is able to respond appropriately to the infant's needs so that the infant is not forced into passive compliance). This is a reversal of the trajectory of the artist and medium, as described by Roussillon above, in which the initially resistant medium becomes malleable in response to the artist's actions. My own view is that the medium is *both* resistant *and* pliable from the beginning of the artist's work with it. Sometimes it seems to conform to the artist's wishes but at other times, perhaps unexpectedly, it throws up problems that the artist must resolve in order to move on.

Roussillon and Wright's contemporary psychoanalytic writing about the pliability and resistance of the artist's medium brings to mind the earlier work of art critic Adrian Stokes. Stokes speculates on the ways in which the artist handles her materials and how this engagement is made manifest in the final work of art. In one of his early works *The Stones of Rimini* (1934), Stokes writes about his personal responses to Italian sculpture, differentiating between two different ways in which artists work with their materials. He calls these 'carving' and 'modelling'. For Stokes, these two modes of working are not merely techniques, they also reflect the artist's attitudes towards and responses to the medium. Stokes sees 'modellers' as using their medium in a 'plastic' way so as to mould it into a preconceived form. The artist imposes her own vision onto her material. According to this formulation, the medium is almost infinitely malleable in its response to the artist's actions. 'Carvers', on the other hand, have regard for the intrinsic properties of the medium and enter into a dialogue with it, struggling with its resistant qualities and taking away from it to reveal the form within:

> Whatever its plastic value, a figure carved in stone is fine carving when one feels that not the figure, but the stone through the medium of the figure, has come to life. Plastic conception, on the other hand, is uppermost when the material with which, or from which, a figure has been made appears no more than as so much suitable stuff for this creation.
>
> *(Stokes 1934: 230)*

Carving establishes the artist's medium as 'out there', as possessing its own characteristics separate from those of the artist. The final artwork arises out of the action of the artist *and* the behavior of the medium in response.

Stokes went on to apply these categories of 'carving' and 'modelling' to other artforms, including painting, suggesting that the carving painter uses colour to reveal the otherness and intrinsic vitality of his canvas: 'The true colourist, then, is recreating by his use of colour the "other", "out-there" vitality he attributes to the surface of the canvas, just as a carver reveals the potential life of the stone' (Stokes 1937: 17).

It is clear from his early writings that Stokes valued carvers more highly than modellers, and in his earlier works he attempted to allocate particular artists to one or other group. However, later he revised his ideas and came to see both modes as necessary for any individual artist when a new artwork is created. All artists must, to some extent, attempt to impose their own ideas onto the medium and all also respond to the particular behaviour of the medium as it responds to their actions.

Stokes was in analysis with Melanie Klein and, following this, he theorised his concepts of 'carving' and 'modelling' in psychoanalytic terms. At this point, I need to say a little about Kleinian theory and its use by psychoanalysts and others in relation to the making of art. Melanie Klein, like Winnicott, focuses on the infant's very early relationships (Klein 1946) and the mental processes that contribute to the building of an inner emotional world. However, unlike Winnicott, she holds that the infant experiences himself as separate from his mother (or primary caregiver) from the beginning of life. She uses the term 'paranoid-schizoid position' for the earliest phase of development when the mother is experienced by the infant as split into good and bad elements (or 'part objects'). The infant loves the good part object (the good breast) and hates the bad part object (the bad breast). According to Klein, later development involves a move towards the 'depressive position' (Klein 1940) in which the infant recognises that the mother is a whole person including both the perceived good and bad elements. The depressive position brings a sense of guilt for the perceived damage done through hateful feelings and phantasies, now recognised to be towards the loved mother, and the sense of what has been lost or damaged gives rise to the desire for reparation (Klein 1929). There is an extensive body of Kleinian literature relating to art and artists, both by psychoanalysts, including Hanna Segal (1952, 1957, 1974, 1978, 1991) and Adela Abella (2007, 2010, 2013), and non-analysts involved in the art world such as the educationalist Anton Ehrenzweig (1948, 1967) and Adrian Stokes. These writers tend to see the artist as engaged in a struggle to restore and rebuild her damaged internal world.

Drawing on Kleinian theory, Stokes links 'carving' with the 'depressive position' and suggests that the carver's respect for the separate identity of the medium corresponds to the relationship with a separate whole object described by Klein. On the other hand, his psychoanalytic formulation of modelling (which owed more to Milner than to Klein) was of a state of oneness between artist and medium.

Stokes' Kleinian theoretical orientation differs from that of Wright and Roussillon, but it is possible to consider his formulation in relation to their ideas. Carving and modelling might be understood as paralleling two aspects of the infant's relationship to the mother. In 'modelling' mode, the artist encounters a malleable 'mother' medium that conforms to her needs, whereas in 'carving' mode, the 'mother' medium is resistant and has to be coerced into a mirroring response.

Although Stokes approaches the topic of the artist's interaction with the medium from his vantage point as an art critic, his later Kleinian formulation emphasises the therapeutic value of the artwork both for artist and viewer. From a different theoretical viewpoint, Wright and Roussillon also highlight this aspect of art-making. In Wright's view, the artist attempts, through art-making, to make good a deficit in the original maternal provision. That is, in so far as the mother or primary caregiver was unable to mirror or be attuned to the infant's gestures, the artist has the opportunity to provide herself with a mirroring or attuning form in the shape of the artwork. In comparing the relationship between artist and medium to that of mother and infant, both Wright and Roussillon see the artist's creative process as an act of self-realisation in which the artist moulds or coerces the medium into becoming a form for her experience. I see this as a central aspect of art-making, and psychoanalysis is particularly well placed to explore this. But this is not all that the artwork has to do. It not only provides an external form for an internal experience but also presents some aspect of the outside world in a new light. The artist moulds or struggles with her medium to create a form that will fulfill *both* these roles.

Roussillon, Wright and Stokes all refer to the artist's medium as if it is the developing artwork itself, but here I want to make a distinction between the two terms. I define the artist's medium as any materials and tools she *uses* in order to make the artwork (including, but not limited to, paint, pencil, stone, wood, clay, found objects, photographs, cameras, film, digital programs, performers, sound). The artist's interaction with her medium is the means through which the developing artwork comes into being as a manifestation in the outside world.

In an interview with Donald Kuspit in 1988, Louise Bourgeois says:

> The material itself, stone or wood, does not interest me as such. It is a means; it is not the end. You do not make sculpture because you like the wood. That is absurd. You make sculpture because the wood allows you to express something that another material does not allow you to do.
>
> *(in Stiles and Selz 2012: 39)*

Bourgeois makes a clear distinction here between the material as the means to an end and the artwork that 'expresses something'. She claims that the material itself does not interest her, but I take this to mean that it interests her only in relation to the potential new artwork. She has chosen this particular material for a reason; she senses its possibilities and has already invested it with something of herself. However, the point of making her sculpture is not to work with stone or wood but to express herself in the final artwork.

This raises the question of whether and how we can distinguish between the medium and the developing work. The photographer's camera or a computer program is clearly a means to make the work rather than a part of it, but the distinction is less clear in the case of materials such as paint, wood or stone, which are themselves transformed into the artwork itself. Some of the interviews, particularly those with painters, indicate that, as the artist works with her materials and tools, there is a point in the process at which a significant change takes place. Whether or not they have an idea for the work in mind, these artists begin to make marks until something happens in the painting and it begins to feel meaningful to them. This is similar to the experience of the painter Frank Auerbach, who feels compelled to repaint until something particular occurs:

> suddenly in the corner of the picture you get a little bit of truth, which might actually expand into a whole truth. You don't know where it's going to come from, you see. What happens is that the painting begins to speak back to one . . . In the end one has stored so many sensations in it that it begins to come alive.
>
> *(in Peppiat 2012: 46)*

This is the point at which the developing artwork, a true reflection of the artist's experience, comes into being.

Francis Bacon, in an interview with Michael Peppiat, says:

> I don't start blind. I have an idea of what I would like to do, but, as I start working, that completely evaporates. If it goes at all well, something will start to crystallize . . . Often you just put on paint almost without knowing what you're doing. You've got to get some material on the canvas to begin with. Then it may or may not begin to work.
>
> *(ibid.: 31)*

Initially, Bacon describes his work simply as 'material on the canvas'. But then something changes. He uses the metaphor of crystallisation to describe this change, the same metaphor used by Simon Faithfull, quoted in Chapter 3, when he speaks about the way a new idea emerges. For both artists, the word seems to denote a coming together, the culmination of a process that has been going on out of their awareness, an emergence of something into consciousness. Bacon downplays the importance of his initial idea, saying that 'It never, never stays that way. It's just to get me into the act of doing it.' The main idea comes later, 'crystallising' as a result of his interaction with his materials. This crystallisation occurs because, as Bacon paints, 'almost without knowing' what he is doing, he brings his own inner experience to bear on the paint. Eventually, this results in a shift from the experience of the paint as a material medium to the paint as an element in a developing artwork.

The philosopher Susanne Langer writes of the difference between 'elements' of a painting and the materials, or medium, used:

> Elements are factors in the semblance; and, as such, they are virtual themselves, direct components of the total form. In this way they differ from materials, which are actual. Paints are materials, and so are the colours they have in the tube or on the palette; but the colours in a picture are elements,

determined by their environment. They are warm or cold, they advance or recede, enhance or soften or dominate other colours; they create tensions and distribute weight in a picture. Colours in a paintbox don't do such things. They are materials and lie side by side in their undialectical materialism.

(Langer 1953: 84–85)

Langer uses the term 'semblance' to refer to the artwork as a 'virtual object' set apart from practical usage. The artist's use of her medium or materials is a process of symbolisation that gives rise to a developing artwork, or, in Langer's terms, a 'semblance'. Langer sees the creation of an artwork as a process of infusing it with 'the dynamism of subjective experience', and she calls this 'vital import'. It is this vital import that gives the sense that the artwork itself is a living force. Langer's ideas about the artist's activity chime closely with my own view that, as the artist works with her medium, she moulds it to reflect her inner experience and, in doing so, imbues it with her own inner life.

From the artist's point of view, there is a point when the developing artwork (no longer merely materials) seems to acquire a life of its own or, in Langer's terms, vital import. Sculptor John Aiken says:

> *Although you know what you're doing, what the result is is something different . . . After a while you've no idea of how you got to where you've got to. What you've got is something that's got its own life, its own energy, and therefore you automatically are in a dialogue with it because it's different. It's not the sum of its parts. It's something rather strange in some cases. You think 'This is an absolutely awful thing that I've made and that wasn't what my intention was or what my aspiration was' . . . But it's kind of interesting . . . That dialogue may very quickly turn into divorce but it's still a dialogue. It's not a romantic notion of a dialogue. It can be a very focused and a very kind of cold dialogue but you are getting something back because you never can predict what's going to happen. So each action is taking a risk, is taking a speculative step.*
>
> *(Aiken 2011)*

Aiken stresses his experience of his artwork as having its own life that is different from him and that therefore opens up a space for dialogue. But, at the same time, he recognises that the artwork tells him something about *himself*, something that he had not previously known. That is, he infuses the work with his own subjective experience so that it takes on something of his own inner life, but the result is a living entity that has its own different character. It reflects his experience *but it also transforms it.* In Bollas' terms, the developing artwork becomes a transformational object that has the power to alter the artist's experience. But this transformational object is not found ready made. Rather, the artist has fashioned it for him- or herself (and for others).

I think that René Roussillon's concept of the 'maternal double', in which he extends Winnicott's theory of maternal mirroring, is relevant here:

> I would nevertheless argue that we have to go beyond Winnicott's hypothesis and see this first 'mirror' as being not only the mother's face but also her entire body and her behaviour . . . This mirror, personified by the mother's body when she is sufficiently adapted to her infant's needs, sufficiently malleable and sensitive towards her infant's internal states, has the effect of producing a narcissistic double (Roussillon 1991). A 'double' is something that is both 'the same' – similar to the self – and also 'an other'. No double can ever be simply the same because that situation would create confusion, rather than a reflection of the self. The mother must therefore show that she is different, an other, through the way in which she reflects to her infant her sharing of emotions. The emotions and internal states that she reflects are similar, but not identical, to those of her infant. They have the same basic components, the same matrix, but not the same form.
>
> *(Roussillon 2010: 830)*

According to Roussillon, the baby is in dialogue with his 'narcissistic double'. That is, his dialogue is with aspects of his own experience, reflected in the mother's face, body and behaviour, but now presented back to him in a form that also reflects something of the mother's different identity. In an analogous way, the developing artwork can be seen as a 'narcissistic double' for the artist in that it gradually comes to embody the artist's inner experience, but this experience is now transformed according to the properties and behaviour of the medium. In addition, if the subject matter of the work is something other than the medium itself, the artist's 'narcissistic double' will also bear the imprint of this subject matter.

5

THE ARTIST'S STATE OF MIND

You know you're alive don't you?. . . . you're engaged really with all of yourself and your senses and you're not taking anything for granted.

Jo Volley

The engagement between artist and medium often calls for the artist to enter a particular state of mind quite different from that of everyday experience. Sculptor George Meyrick puts it this way:

> *You're buried in what you're doing. The outside world doesn't intrude. It just makes a big difference that you are not disturbed by other thoughts coming through . . . It's very intense and concentrated . . . So there'll be, you know, the kind of 'let's tidy up and sweep up and make a cup of tea' kind of stuff but it's not displacement activity it's – I don't know – circling around and then . . . You sort of pounce on a possibility – something just kind of gives an opening gambit to how you might approach something and then, once that happens, the concentration, intensity, increases exponentially . . . It does get like a sort of welding torch – a sort of white heat of something there. You're right in it and you're not thinking about anything else except how this will go, what might happen.*
>
> *(Meyrick 2012)*

Meyrick describes a very intense experience, and he gives some clues about the ways in which he sets up the conditions to enter this state. The outside world must not distract him but, more than that, his own thoughts about other matters must be banished too. The tidying or sweeping or making tea seem to have the function of setting the scene and of providing a space into which a 'possibility' might emerge. His description of 'circling round' and 'pouncing' suggests that this possibility is elusive and must be captured immediately whilst the metaphor of the sculptor's welding torch conveys an image of highly concentrated creative energy.

Another interviewee, Sian Bonnell, describes her state of mind while working:

> *Whenever I make my work, when I do get into it, I do go into this strange place which sounds a bit odd but it's almost trancelike. It does become trancelike . . . I can describe it as very sure of yourself and what you're doing even though you know afterwards it might not be a good piece of work . . . If I'm in a really good zone it's right in there, it's all about my real innermost me. It's really connecting with what is real, really real . . . I don't eat, I don't drink . . . I couldn't stop. I would lose it. You have to stay in it.*
>
> *(Bonnell 2011)*

Again, this artist's description conveys the intensity of her experience. She is completely focused on her work and very 'sure' of herself, suggesting that, for the time being, any internal criticisms are suspended so that she can allow the work to progress without interruption. Her use of the phrase 'in a really good zone' connects her experience with that of musicians, sports persons and many others who feel immersed in an activity. The psychologist Mihály Csíkszentmihályi has studied these experiences and coined the term 'flow' for a state in which someone is narrowly focused on a particular activity (Csíkszentmihályi 1996). In this state, the person is immersed in the present moment, loses reflective self-consciousness, has a sense of personal agency or control over the activity they are engaged in, experiences the activity as intrinsically rewarding and has an altered experience of time. Bonnell's description, and that of other interviewees, many of whom said that they lost track of time whilst working, is congruent with Csíkszentmihályi's definition of 'flow'. But there is something more in Bonnell's statement. She says that in this state she feels connected with something 'real' and with her 'innermost me'. I understand this to mean that she is in a state in which the boundaries between inner and outer worlds are attenuated. Her 'innermost me' is that element of her internal world that was activated by the aesthetic process. Her use of her medium allows her to translate her 'innermost me' into the artwork.

Dryden Goodwin describes his experience of drawing on a photograph in his studio:

> *It was about the drag of the drawing device on the drawing surface. That set up a physical sensation that put me in a certain state. Or if I was wearing a magnifier the sense of my body behind my eyes would dissolve and a sort of . . . intimacy would develop . . . In the studio I have to be in a certain state . . . it's about being very involved. What's very schematic, very structural in its approach is then set aside as you become involved in that pocket you've created to lose yourself in the activity.*
>
> *(Goodwin 2011)*

Again, this artist describes a state that corresponds with Csíkszentmihályi's concept of 'flow'. Like Meyrick and Bonnell, Goodwin is in a state of deep involvement, different from the state he is in at other times but, again, this seems to me to be an experience over and above that of 'flow'. In order to enter this state, he has to relinquish his previous schematic way of thinking and move into another space (a 'pocket') that he has set up for himself. I will come back to his use of the word 'pocket' in Chapter 9, but here I want to consider what Goodwin might mean by 'intimacy' and how his interaction with his medium – the drawing device, drawing surface and magnifier – enables this to develop.

In order to explore the nature of this 'intimacy', I turn to Marion Milner's writing about the state that she calls 'illusion'. In her paper 'The Role of Illusion in Symbol Formation' (1952a), Milner describes her clinical work with a young boy and the way in which the boy used her as a pliable medium that would respond to his commands. Milner found that the boy treated her as if she were a part of himself that he could control and direct. Over time, she recognised that this was a necessary stage in his development:

> Thus a central idea began to emerge about what this boy was trying to tell me; it was the idea that the basic identifications which make it possible to find new objects, to find the familiar in the unfamiliar, require an ability to tolerate a temporary loss of sense of self, a temporary giving up of the discriminating ego which stands apart and tries to see things objectively and rationally and without emotional colouring.
>
> *(ibid.: 97)*

Through her work with the boy, Milner understood that his behaviour was not merely a defensive regression. Rather, by allowing him to be in a state of 'illusion' in which there is a felt state of oneness between self and object (in this case, between the boy and her as object), she set the scene for his development towards an experience of 'twoness' and the ability to symbolise. Milner went on to compare the state of illusion that might occur in psychoanalysis with that experienced by the artist. She writes:

> Could one say that by finding a bit of the outside world, whether in chalk or paper, or in one's analyst, that was willing temporarily to fit in with one's dreams, a moment of illusion was made possible, a moment in which inner and outer seemed to coincide?
>
> *(Milner 1957: 119)*

Milner's concept of illusion as a coincidence of inner and outer, a merging of artist and medium, seems to speak to Goodwin's sense of his body 'dissolving'. His physical interaction with the drawing surface (that is, the boundary between himself and the work) sets the scene whilst the magnifier seems to draw him inside the work itself. He goes on to say:

> *There's meaning in the method for me. Because within this process of starting to make the mark there's a sense of pushing through the illusionary space of the photograph . . .*

back into this four dimensional space that the photograph was taken in . . . in a sense I then became enveloped within the sense of this person, within the image . . . the drawing was somehow allowing my imagination to fully enter the image. And then I become absorbed in that activity so I'm no longer self-conscious, I'm involved and contained within this interaction between myself and this individual as captured by this photograph. So the specifics of how that drawing goes is totally determined by that experience.

(Goodwin 2011)

It seems that the artist experiences the two-dimensional photograph as too separate, excluding him. He wants to get inside it, to push through the surface, as if by doing so he can be enveloped in the space–time moment of the image. His use of words such as 'enveloped', 'absorbed', 'fully enter' and 'involved and contained' seems to relate to Milner's concept of illusion. He says that he is 'no longer self-conscious', by which I understand him to mean that his consciousness of himself as a person separate from the individual in the photograph is in abeyance. He bridges the gap (in fantasy) between himself and the person photographed in order to attempt to create an artwork that will embody the essence of this person *as he experiences it*. The artist expresses a desire to achieve a 'truer' representation by connecting more closely to a sense of the person photographed. To do so, he must somehow get inside that person, to inhabit them from the inside and sense what it is like to be them. But this identification is with the person as they appear in his photograph, and he has already imbued this image with aspects of his own inner world. He chose this particular photograph because he sensed that it held some significance for him personally, and his process of drawing changes the photograph in ways that reflect his own experience. Through his physical work on the photograph, he aims to identify more and more closely with the person in the image whilst, at the same time, recognising and embracing the fact that his intervention inevitably influences his sense of that person. As he works, the developing artwork comes to embody and symbolise both the person photographed and the artist's inner experience.

So far I have discussed the state of mind of the artist who is absorbed in her work, a state that seems to correspond with Milner's state of 'illusion'. But interviewees also describe more focused states in which moment-to-moment decisions can be made:

It's oscillating between being very conscious – because you've got to make practical decisions – and being very intuitive and reactive.

(Goodwin 2011)

Goodwin describes an alternation between two states of mind, one in which he makes decisions about how to move forward in the work and the other, which he seems to see as less 'conscious', as more intuitive. Another artist, John Aiken, describes his experience in this way:

I would say it's like heightened reality and being in a trance at one and the same time. So you become totally absorbed in something which could be very mundane and at the same time your thoughts are racing and you're making lots of decisions and you're going forward and you're going back and you're unpicking it and you're developing it and you're imaging something.

(Aiken 2011)

This artist again distinguishes between two different states of mind, but suggests that his experience of 'trance' or total absorption occurs 'at the same time' as the sense of heightened reality in which he can make decisions. This raises the question of whether this should be taken literally or whether he is describing fluctuations in his state of mind that are so rapid or so subtle that they do not interrupt his absorption in his work.

To explore this question, I want to turn to the work of Anton Ehrenzweig, a lecturer in art education at Goldsmith's College, London. Ehrenzweig developed a three-phase model of the artist's creative process (Ehrenzweig 1967) based on Kleinian psychoanalytic theory. Ehrenzweig argues that the creation of a work of art can be regarded as an attempt to integrate 'unacknowledged split-off elements of the self' (ibid.: 102). He suggests that in the first phase of the artist's process (which he links with Klein's theory of the paranoid-schizoid position), she projects fragmented and split-off parts of herself into the work. In the second ('manic') phase, a process of unconscious scanning takes place that aims towards integration. Ehrenzweig writes: 'creative dedifferentiation tends towards a manic "oceanic" limit where all differentiation ceases. The inside and outside world begin to merge. . . . .' (ibid.: 103). In this phase, the persecutory anxieties of the first phase recede as distinctions are blurred and the fragmentation seems to be resolved. Ehrenzweig contends that most of the creative work takes place in this phase whilst the artist is in this 'dedifferentiated' state of mind. This gives way to a more realistic evaluation in the third phase when the artist acknowledges the gaps and fragmentation that were ignored earlier. Ehrenzweig links this third phase to Klein's 'depressive position'. The acknowledgement of limitations paves the way for a process of secondary revision and the final result, although not necessarily a complete resolution of the initial fragmentation, becomes an 'unbroken pictorial space' in which different fragments are bound together.

Ehrenzweig defines dedifferentiation as 'the dynamic process by which the ego scatters and represses surface imagery' and links it with 'syncretistic vision' through which all the elements of an artwork can be taken in at once:

There must be an unconscious undifferentiated type of visualization which is free from the compulsion of bisecting the visual field in terms of figure and ground and can scan it in its entirety with impartial equality.

(Ehrenzweig 1962: 1010)

Dedifferentiation is the process by which the artist adopts this mode of seeing. It involves a broadening, or 'flexible scattering', of attention and an 'unconscious scanning' which includes all the diverse elements of the work at once. Ehrenzweig sees this mode of seeing as alternating with a more focused mode in which elements of the work are differentiated, so that the artist's process involves a 'smooth oscillation between focused and unfocused modes of perception' (Ehrenzweig 1967: 28). So far, Ehrenzweig seems to present two different ways of *seeing*, but in his book *The Hidden Order of Art*, he takes the concept of dedifferentiation beyond the purely visual and writes of the artist's creative process as a 'fruitful alternation between differentiated and undifferentiated modes of functioning' (ibid.: 35).

Ehrenzweig's discussion of the artist's process as an oscillation between two modes of seeing and functioning has much in common with the writing of Marion Milner. In her book *On Not Being Able to Paint*, Milner describes her attempts to paint in terms of a struggle between two ways of seeing (Milner 1957: 21). The academic John Turner describes her book as:

> an account of her struggle as a painter to help her eye escape the tyranny of edge and outline. It was a struggle, she thought, between two kinds of seeing: a kind of denotative, or objective seeing, necessary to perceive the otherness of the created world in all its difference from the self, and a kind of poetic, or oceanic seeing, necessary to suffuse the otherness of the outside world with the sense of self. Both kinds of seeing, she believed, belonged to human beings, and both were necessary. Objective seeing helped to establish our sense of separateness as human beings, while poetic seeing reaffirmed powerful infantile experiences of fusion, before the boundary line between inner and outer was drawn, when the breast that satisfied and the hunger that was satisfied were one.
>
> *(Turner 2002: 1070)*

Here, Turner points out how Milner links this latter type of seeing with very early infantile experiences, a time when the infant did not yet experience himself as a being separate from his mother and the world around him. This type of seeing goes hand in hand with the state of 'illusion' or 'oneness' described by Milner as integral to art-making.

Milner was a contemporary of Ehrenzweig's and was in agreement with him about what she describes as:

> the role in art of that inherent capacity of the ego's awareness which causes it to swing between conscious, directed, deliberative attention, and an absent-minded dream-like state, in a kind of porpoise-like movement of emergence and submergence.
>
> *(Milner 1967: 242)*

Both Milner and Ehrenzweig regard the artist's process as an alternation between two very different states of mind and seem to suggest that, at any one moment, the artist is *either* in one mode *or* the other.

But, in the paper I quote from above, Turner goes on to question whether Milner's separation of these two ways of seeing can be maintained, writing: 'I do not want to deny either the utility or the truth of Milner's typology but rather to ask whether difference is the only relationship that we can imagine between her two kinds of thinking and seeing. Need we think only in terms of either/or?' (Turner 2002: 1071). Taking Turner's question further, I am not convinced that the concept of an alternation between two states of mind is fully compatible with the experiences of the artists I interviewed. I want to explore here whether there may be another way of thinking about the artist's experience.

I will begin with the terminology that Milner employs when writing about the state she calls 'illusion'. She seems to use the terms 'illusion', 'oneness' and 'fusion' interchangeably, and it is the term 'fusion' that I want to question here. This word implies a complete lack of differentiation between self and object, as if there is no 'I' to observe the interaction. Milner herself did not intend to suggest that art-making involves a complete loss of self and, indeed, she does write of the fear that the state of oneness or fusion might go too far: '. . . even if it were true that one did need, at times, not to have to decide which was the other and which was oneself, such a state obviously had its dangers. It might become so alluring that one did not wish to return to the real world of being separate' (Milner 1957: 31). The allure of the illusionary state of fusion harks back to the experience of the infant at the breast, a pre-separation experience that is both enticing and threatening. Milner describes a fear of becoming lost in the illusionary state, of being unable to regain her sense of separateness. This implies that, unless the state tips into one of psychosis, the artist does retain some vestige of a sense of separateness, even whilst in the state of 'illusion' or 'oneness'. The difference between the artist's experience and that of the infant is that the infant has not yet reached a state of separate identity, has not yet become a subject in his own right. The artist's intimacy with the developing artwork may be a recapitulation of this early state of oneness, but it is usually experienced from the adult position of having already established a more reliable sense of separate identity (although this difference between artist and infant may not always be clear cut. If the artist's sense of identity was not firmly established at an earlier stage of life, she may also be engaged in a developmental task.)

If, when in a state of 'illusion', the artist retains some sense of her separate self, Milner and Ehrenzweig's picture of an alternation between two different states seems to need modification. Milner writes that while painting, 'something quite special happened to one's sense of self' (Milner 1957: 142). I now want to examine what it is that happens to the artist's sense of self as she works. To explore this, I turn to my own recent experience of making a new photography-based installation, *The Transience of Wonder*. My work on this piece began several years ago. I knew that I wanted to make a work that would embody something of my experience of climbing mountains in the Cumbrian Lake District. I could not pinpoint exactly what it was that I wanted to capture, but I knew that it had something to do with the sky as viewed when one looks vertically upwards. In the terms

I use in this book, I had a 'pre-sense' to do with my experience of the sky on the Cumbrian mountains. I therefore began to take photographs as I climbed, stopping at regular intervals and directing my camera to the sky immediately above my head. I then printed 'slices' of these photographs and juxtaposed them into a timeline of the journey I took (see Figure 5.1).

As I worked on this, I felt absorbed in my attempt to infuse the work with something of the inner experience I wanted to embody. At this point, I did feel a sense of oneness with the developing work. However, in retrospect, it did not seem to me that I moved out of that state in order to make moment-to-moment decisions about such practical questions as how to manipulate the photographs or the colour balance of the print. Only when the print was finished did I look more objectively at it. At that point, I felt that it was not capturing my experience well enough. Over an extended period, I tried many different configurations and used photographs from walks on several different mountains. As I worked on each successive incarnation of the work, I entered a state of mind in which I was fully absorbed or, to use Aiken's expression from the quotation above, 'in a trance', but, *at the same time*, I was making practical decisions. Indeed, I could only make appropriate decisions if I retained my close connection, or sense of 'oneness', with the work, as I needed to sense whether the changes I made brought it closer to, or further from, my inner experience. The essence of this close connection was the need to stay in touch with this inner experience through my pre-sense. That is, the sense of oneness could be thought of as a resonance between a particular element of my inner world – that element that had responded to my experience whilst in the mountains – and the developing artwork. I had to hold the memory of my pre-sense in mind as I worked with my medium so that I could mould it into a form that would 'fit' my inner experience and so evoke it or recreate it (I return to this piece of work and its later form in Chapter 10).

From the analysis of my own process and the evidence of the interviewees, I think that, whilst working with her medium, the artist enters a state of mind in which she is *both* at one with the developing work *and* able to focus on details, although one or other state will be to the fore at any particular moment. This state can be thought of as a continuum between two experiences of the self that I will call the artist's 'extended self' and 'observer self'. The 'extended self' refers to an extension of the boundaries of self-experience to include the developing artwork. The 'observer self' refers to the artist's capacity to focus on the

FIGURE 5.1 *The Transience of Wonder.* Work in progress 1

moment-to-moment practical ways in which the artwork can be developed further. The two aspects of the artist's self-experience are necessary to each other, operating in tandem as the artist works to coerce her medium to provide a form for her experience. Through the 'extended self', that is by the loosening of the boundaries between self and object, the artist relates to the developing artwork as if it is becoming that part of her inner experience that she wants it to embody. But it can only become a form for this inner experience if the 'observer self', responding to the 'extended self', directs the artist to make appropriate changes to the developing work. There is, therefore, a continuous interchange between the 'extended self' and the 'observer self', although, at any one moment, one or other will be uppermost.

These new terms address the objections that have been raised to Milner's use of the word 'fusion' when writing of the artist's state of mind (Eigen 1983). In the formulation I put forward, there is never a total fusion between the artist and the developing artwork (except in psychosis). The sense of 'oneness' experienced in the 'extended self' mode is always tempered by the co-existence of the 'observer self'.

The terms 'extended self' and 'observer self' have something in common with Christopher Bollas' terms 'simple self' (when we are immersed in an experience) and 'complex self' (when we reflect upon experience) (Bollas 1992c). However, Bollas' terms refer to all self-experiencing, whereas the terms I introduce are specific to the process of making art. The new terms can also be related to Stokes' modes of 'modelling' and 'carving' discussed in Chapter 4. Stokes saw the 'modelling' artist as in a state of oneness with the medium (or, I would say, the developing artwork) and this corresponds to the 'extended self' mode. He saw the 'carving' artist as relating to the medium as separate from herself, and this parallels the mode of 'observer self'.

In states when the artist's 'extended self' is uppermost, the sense of losing oneself in the work can be an intense experience. However, this very intensity may at times be extremely frightening, as Deborah Padfield describes:

> *Suddenly I have to have this when my brain slips. It feels like the lid coming off . . .*
> *It's like an intense living . . . The creative process, for me when it's really coming to*
> *fruition at the end of the piece, that to me is intensity but it also feels like real living.*
> *I feel like I'm me, I'm alive, and that something very real and intense is going on.*
> *At that point it's not really enjoyable. There's something quite dangerous and there's*
> *something quite urgent about it and it feels as though something is at stake but quite*
> *what is at stake and why one gets into this state where so much is at stake I don't*
> *know . . . At that point the right decision seems to be so vital.*
>
> *(Padfield 2011)*

I think that the danger felt by Padfield, and also described by other interviewees, is the fear of a permanent state of 'losing' herself in the work, of no longer being able to separate out. However, Padfield says that the right decision seems vital, indicating that she is still able to make decisions about the work. The capacity to think and make decisions is primarily a function of the 'observer self', so the danger here seems to be the possibility of losing touch with her 'observer self'. In the 'extended self' state, the artist responds in a sensual, pre-symbolic way to the developing work whilst the 'observer self' functions at a more symbolic level, organising experience and responding to the developing work within a wider context. Looked at in this way, the threat of becoming lost in the state of 'illusion' can be understood as a fear of losing one's symbolising capacity.

By introducing the concept of a continuum between the extended self-state and the observer self-state, I do not want to suggest that there cannot be fleeting moments when the observer self-state seems to disappear completely. Such moments are described by poets, including T.S. Eliot, Gerard Manley Hopkins and William Wordsworth, but are not the prerogative of artists and creative writers. Experiences in the landscape or while listening to music or gazing at a painting can engender an ecstatic sense of oneness. These brief moments may also occur during the making of an artwork. But the argument I want to make is that experiences of ecstatic union are not essential to the artist's process. It is the movement along the continuum between the deep involvement of the 'extended self' and the more focused 'observer self' that enables the development of the work.

6

PLAY AND PLAYING

Sometimes it's an accident that allows something else to happen. That's generally why I have to play a lot.

Gina Glover

Making art involves hard work. The artist engages in research and experimentation, sources materials, works with her medium, liaises with commissioners, explores venues and so on. But an aspect of some phases of this work, particularly the phase of working with the medium, can also be seen as a form of serious play. Winnicott wrote about the nature of play and playing at various points over the course of his writing career. His early writing derived from his analytic work with children, but he emphasises that everything he writes about children's playing also applies to adults. Play, he argues, is a creative activity that is 'universal' and 'natural', contributing to growth and health. In his paper 'Why Children Play' he writes:

> The repressed unconscious must be kept hidden, but the rest of the unconscious is something that each individual wants to get to know, and play, like dreams, serves the function of self-revelation.
>
> (Winnicott 1942: 146)

Winnicott does not often use the terms 'conscious' and 'unconscious', preferring to write of the outer and inner world. But here, specifically referring to the unrepressed unconscious, he sees play as a means of accessing the unconscious. There is a parallel between the function Winnicott ascribes to play and one of the functions of making art. In this book, I develop the idea that the creation of a new artwork is (amongst other things) a search for a form for something hitherto unformed in the artist's inner world. This search, as an activity, can be seen as play in Winnicott's sense of the word. The new artwork embodies something in the unrepressed unconscious, and in doing so it allows the artist to 'get to know' this aspect of herself.

Winnicott's later writings about play owe a great deal to the development of his theory of transitional phenomena. He came to see play as situated on a continuum between the infant's use of the transitional object and the adult's involvement in cultural activity. All these activities take place in an intermediate area of experiencing, a potential space, where inner and outer worlds exist simultaneously. In his paper 'Playing: Its Theoretical Status in the Clinical Situation', Winnicott writes:

> I tried to make my idea of play concrete by claiming that *playing has a place* and a time. It is not *inside* by any use of the word . . . Nor is it *outside*, that is to say, it is not a part of the repudiated world, the not–me, that which the individual has decided to recognize (with whatever difficulty and even pain) as truly external, outside magical control. To control what is outside one has to *do* things, not simply to think or to wish, and *doing things takes time*. Playing is doing.
>
> *(Winnicott 1968: 592)*

In this paper, he pays tribute to Milner's reference to play in her paper 'The Role of Illusion in Symbol Formation' (1952a) where she writes that apparent regression in play may be a necessary stage in a creative relation to the world. To play, in Milner and Winnicott's view, is to endow some aspect of the outside world with inner experience and then to interact with this 'subjective object' in a creative way. For the infant, play takes place in the potential space between mother and child; in psychoanalysis or psychotherapy, the potential space is between analyst and patient:

> Psychotherapy takes place in the overlap of two areas of playing, that of the patient and that of the therapist. Psychotherapy has to do with two people playing together. The corollary of this is that where playing is not possible then the work done by the therapist is directed towards bringing the patient from a state of not being able to play into a state of being able to play.
>
> *(Winnicott 1986b: 44)*

The psychoanalyst Michael Parsons explores the implications of Winnicott's statement in his paper 'The Logic of Play in Psychoanalysis' (1999), writing: 'The play element is not just an occasional aspect of analysis, but functions continuously to sustain a paradoxical reality where things can be real and not real at the same time. This paradox is the framework of psychoanalysis' (ibid.: 871). It is also the framework of the artist's relationship with her medium, as I will explore in this chapter.

I will start with my own process of making one of the pieces in the More-cambe Bay series of works:

> *I was fascinated by the rapid changes in the Bay as the tide swept in or out, the in-between state of the landscape when it was both land and sea. The idea came to me of making a print in which two blocks of text, one ochre and one blue, overlapped each other, creating an intermediate space. From this beginning the piece evolved through a number of transformations or reincarnations as I tried numerous variations in the text. I also experimented with different fonts and text layouts, changing these repeatedly until it seemed 'right'. I was not entirely sure what I wanted the text to do. Initially I thought that I wanted the ochre text to relate to the outside world and the blue to the inner world and, with this in mind, I tried various alternatives. I tried using dream narratives and their interpretations and then single repeated words. I rejected each attempt as somehow unsatisfactory and further ideas came to my mind. In the final version, the blue text is composed of words related to my emotional responses to the Bay and the ochre text is related to my responses to the nearby mountains.*

This experimentation with different texts, colours and fonts can be seen as a form of play in which I used my medium to try out different approaches, attempting to sense whether each variation was closer to, or further from, the inner experience I wanted to embody in the work. In trying out different configurations, I was assessing each variation not only in terms of whether or not it satisfied criteria of which I was aware but also whether it 'felt right' at a less conscious level. I was actively manipulating my medium, something in the outside world, according to inner promptings. This activity corresponds with Winnicott's notion of play.

As I discuss above, Winnicott stresses the similarities between the activities of the infant with the transitional object and the older child or adult's play. But there are also differences, as Ken Wright explains:

> [Play] lies further along the path of symbolic formation than the moment of the transitional object. Winnicott has bracketed together play and transitional experience and this may have obscured the differences between the play object and the transitional object itself. That difference is profound and critical and lies in the degree to which the pattern in the object is felt to be separate and separable from a single object. In the transitional object, the pattern inheres in that single object and in no other (except the original one); in play, by contrast, the pattern is freely transferable from object to object.
>
> *(Wright 1991: 248)*

The infant's teddy bear or blanket is inextricably linked, for the infant, with his mother and is irreplaceable. The 'pattern' in the plaything or the art object, on the other hand, could be constituted in a variety of different ways. Here, Wright uses the term 'pattern' in the same way as the word 'form' is used by Langer (and by Wright himself in other contexts). The pattern, or form, becomes a more symbolic representation as the separateness from the object increases.

My play with different texts and colours was a long and frustrating process. There was an inherent difficulty in my decision to use text, in that I was trying to capture an experience that could not be put into words so that each attempt seemed to pin the work down too much. As I experimented, I realised that I did not want to use text consisting of coherent narratives as their meaning seemed too fixed. My experience could not be expressed in the discursive symbols of language. Rather, I needed to *show* how it was in the form of a presentational symbol, or 'semblance' (Langer 1957). Therefore I chose to use a succession of single words in place of a narrative. In the ochre text these words ran smoothly, but in the blue text they were interrupted by gaps and repeated punctuation marks so that the text itself took on the qualities of an image.

Eventually I produced the print. But I was disappointed. It seemed to me to be too static, not reflecting the fluid nature of the tidal movement. For a while, I felt stuck again but then the idea emerged of reworking the piece as an animation and editing it so that the two blocks of text moved over one another. Again I experimented to achieve the particular movement and speed that felt right. After much trial and error, I created a wavelike motion that captured something of the effect I wanted.

(See Figure 6.1.)

The process of play continued here but with a different medium. No longer pen on paper or typed text, my medium here was a digital animation program, and it was this that I struggled with to achieve the effect I wanted. Again, it was a

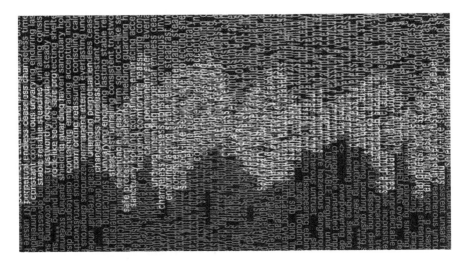

FIGURE 6.1 *Bay Mountain.* HD video animation, work in progress

tortuous process in which I often felt like giving up altogether. Having created the animation, I was still dissatisfied:

> *Now it seemed too flat and I wanted to introduce a third dimension. Again, I could not immediately see a way through this impasse. Eventually I had the idea of projecting the animation onto a 'mountain range' of sand.*
>
> *(See Figure 6.2.)*

In the last stage of play for this piece, I introduced yet another medium in the form of the sand. I brought something related to the physical substance of the Bay into the gallery and the ephemeral video became a physical mass, seemingly solid but actually shifting and unreliable. At last I felt that it did relate closely enough to my experience. When this piece was exhibited, I discovered another, unforeseen, movement in it. As the sand dried out over the course of the exhibition, the 'mountain range' began to crumble and slip. This unpredictable movement seemed to me to add something to the work.

In using the term 'play' to describe my interaction with the sand and with all the other elements of my medium, I do not want to suggest that my activity was always enjoyable. In order to find the form I needed, I had to be in touch with the disturbing feelings that the Bay evokes in me. Each time I tried a new variation, I needed to measure it against my experience. In addition, if something did not 'feel right' I was disappointed and frustrated, and I had to tolerate these feelings too, not knowing whether or not another way forward would emerge. Considering

FIGURE 6.2 *Bay Mountain*. Sand, HD video animation. Slade Research Centre, 2009

these various stages in relation to Wright's quotation above, I played with different forms, transferring my experience from one to the next until I was satisfied that I had found the closest possible 'fit'.

One of the interviewees, Gina Glover, describes her work as a form of play:

> *I am very interesting in playing … I'm a photographer and so my camera is my tool and I will have made a decision before I begin about whether the piece (if it is eventually going to be a piece) is going to be done with a certain piece of equipment to begin with. I often use a pinhole camera… but even before that there's a sort of play action whereby I'm not sure what equipment I might be using. . . . Although I go at the start of the residency with some particular idea to get me started.… throughout my time I would be playing so there would be a whole lot of photographs that I just take with no idea if they are ever going to go anywhere.… I know what I'm looking for but I know it's going to shift.*
>
> *(Glover 2011)*

Glover's initial 'idea' is an image of a possible work, but it is provisional. It initiates a series of experiments, both in her imagination and in the outside world. To begin with, there is the 'play' of the decision about which equipment to use. In imagination she plays with the idea of using a pinhole camera. Would this give the effect she wants? If not, should she use a digital camera or a large-format one? This may lead her to try out different equipment and compare the results before making a decision, or she may choose on the basis of her experience and her imaginative 'playing' with likely effects. Having chosen her equipment, she then moves on to a different sort of experimentation, this time with taking the photographs themselves. She 'plays' not only with the subject matter of her images but also with angle, lighting, framing and so on:

> *There's a whole lot of processes I give myself. Have I looked at this building from the other side? It's a really good discipline to do … It's this whole business of trying to make work with fresh eyes . . . by either calming the brain and letting the brain become empty and therefore the eyes see something differently or you're just allowing the eyes to see what you're trying to make by a different light, by different locations.*
>
> *(Glover 2011)*

Each new cast of the light or each angle of shot is judged not only technically but also in terms of whether or not the effect furthers the developing artwork and feels 'right' (in the terms of this book, whether it is consistent with the artist's pre-sense). Having taken her photographs, yet another period of 'play' follows. She must edit them. Another photographer, Sian Bonnell, describes her method of editing:

> *I put everything on the wall – cheap prints – and don't even look at it. I live with it for a week or two and every night I'll just pick one off … I'll suddenly look at it*

one day and I'll think: 'Oh what's happened there? That doesn't work'… and take it out. And that's how I do it [until] I've got it to a stage where you can see that something is happening with them all working with the others.

(Bonnell 2011)

This artist exhibits her work as a series of photographic images. The finished artwork does not consist in any single image but in their cumulative impact. They have to 'work together' to produce the effect (an effect that reflects her inner experience), and if any one image fails to contribute to the whole, it must be taken out. The quotations above are from photographers, but all the artists described experimentation with their medium, and it is this experimentation that I refer to as play, following Winnicott's use of the term.

In a summary of his thoughts about play, Winnicott writes:

> This area of playing is not inner psychic reality. It is outside the individual, but it is not the external world… into this play area the child gathers objects or phenomena from external reality and uses these in the service of some sample derived from inner or personal reality. Without hallucinating the child puts out a sample of dream potential and lives with this sample in a chosen setting of fragments from external reality. … In playing, the child manipulates external phenomena in the service of the dream and invests chosen external phenomena with dream meaning and feeling.
>
> *(Winnicott 1986b: 60)*

Winnicott sees play (and, by extension, artistic activity) as rooted in the 'dream'. Here, I understand 'the dream' to refer to inner fantasy and 'a sample of dream potential' to be an aspect of internal fantasy that is to be elaborated in play. Considering the artist's play in the light of this, the 'objects or phenomena from external reality' are the artist's medium and subject matter. The question of exactly what the 'sample of dream potential' relates to, in the terms I use here, is more complex. Winnicott's use of the word 'potential' links closely with my definition of the artist's pre-sense in Chapter 1. The pre-sense heralds the potential of a particular aspect of the outside world (in Winnicott's words, a 'fragment of external reality') to offer a route towards a form for something internal. However, I argue that the pre-sense is still vague and unformed. Winnicott's reference to dream suggests something that already has the beginnings of a form, and therefore I think that it relates more closely to the 'idea' in my formulation than to the pre-sense. This interpretation of Winnicott's language is consistent with the way in which Christopher Bollas links creative activity to dream. He writes that 'the total dream process is very likely the cornerstone of the creative, a movement of the "to be represented" towards the fulfilment of this desire' (Bollas 1999: 170). Here, he seems to be referring to the 'creation' of a dream in the process of psychic genera leading to an idea, as I discussed in Chapter 2.

Winnicott highlights the physical nature of play. It involves the body and 'the manipulation of objects' and 'certain types of intense interest are associated with certain aspects of bodily excitement' (Winnicott 1968) (by this definition, the artist's imaginative manipulation of ideas would not come under the heading of 'play'). Of the artists interviewed, painters were most likely to mention the physical pleasure of using their materials:

> *I'm interested in material ... it's very important to my process ... I really feel my process in a really physical way ... which is a very nice feeling ... you know it's in tune with what's going on in your head. It's more the physical, the mental sensuality of it ... the making, as it all comes together ... So that's very exciting.*
>
> *(Volley 2011)*

Jo Volley is speaking both about her sensual enjoyment of her materials and about the moment when her physical actions seem in close accord with 'what's going on in your head'. Although this connection with the physical may be more to the fore for painters or sculptors, it is present for all artists. When I work with the computer, I am familiar with the way I need to move the mouse and the way an image on the screen may differ from the printed image and so on. And, like Volley, I feel excited when these physical impressions are linked with the sense that the movements I make are in tune with what is going on in my head.

Robert Caper, a Kleinian psychoanalyst, writes that play by both children and adults is 'a serious type of experimentation' by means of which one learns about the internal and external worlds. He writes: 'play is a way of externalising fantasies originating in one's inner world so they may be seen and learned about' (Caper 1996: 859). He goes on to write:

> when children play, they are not just testing the world to see what it is like, they are also externalising their internal fantasy world. I say 'externalising' rather than 'representing' because play is more than a representation of unconscious fantasy. It is a way of getting something from inside to outside so we can see what it is, in the spirit of E. M. Forster's question, 'how do I know what I think until I've had a chance to hear what I have to say?'
>
> *(ibid.: 861)*

Caper insists that for this process to 'work properly', 'internal and external reality must be kept separate in one's mind'. According to him, the externalisation of the inner something in play can only go smoothly if the difference between inside and outside is clear. However, later in his paper, he writes:

> Awareness of the mutual autonomy of external and internal realities creates a space or gap in which one may 'play' with external reality without feeling that one's fantasies have had too great an effect on it (so that we are not inhibited in our creative or experimental play). At the same time, this gap

keeps our fantasies safe from too much of an impact of external reality, so we are still free to imagine.

(ibid.: 867)

This is close to Winnicott's concept of potential space. Rather than the clear separation between inner and outer that he writes about earlier in his paper, here Caper seems to be talking about a 'gap' between the two within which an overlap can occur. According to Winnicott, play and all creative activity takes place in the potential space between inner and outer worlds. For the artist, this potential space is between herself and her medium, but also between herself and whatever aspect of the outer world she wishes to explore in her work.

Rather than a keeping separate of inner and outer, as Caper suggests early in his paper, I suggest that the artist's 'play' requires *both* a separation between *and* an overlap of internal and external reality. Relating this to the discussion in Chapter 5 of the artist's two modes of functioning of 'extended self' and 'observer self', and the continuum between the two, the 'extended self' relates to the overlap of internal and external whilst the 'observer self' relates to their separation. For the artist at work, both states exist simultaneously.

In this chapter, I have been concerned with Winnicott's notion of 'play' and its relevance to the artist's process. This play is often enjoyable but it is also a serious, and sometimes painful, business. Following Winnicott, Joyce McDougall, a member of the Paris Psychoanalytical Society who weaves together elements from Freudian, Kleinian, Lacanian and Winnicottian schools, also uses the term 'play' for adult creative activity. She acknowledges the pain and work involved, but goes further:

> Although both Freud and Winnicott advanced the notion that creativity involves playing, this must not be taken to mean that creative activity is carefree. On the contrary, creative or innovative activity of any kind is invariably associated with considerable violence and frequently arouses intense experiences of anguish and guilt.
>
> *(McDougall 1995: 55)*

Play in creative activity, according to McDougall, always involves violence and destructiveness. In the next chapter, I will consider what this might mean in the context of the artist's process.

7

CREATIVITY, AGGRESSION AND DESTRUCTIVENESS

I think it's where destructivity and creativity are quite close. It's on that intersect. One doesn't work for me without the other.

Deborah Padfield

The artist Cornelia Parker often creates works that involve destroying objects in order to recreate them in a very different form. For one of her most impressive works *Cold Dark Matter: An Exploded View* (Parker 1991), she arranged for a shed containing various objects to be blown up. She then created an installation in which the resulting fragments were suspended in the centre of a gallery room. In another work, *30 Pieces of Silver* (Parker, 1988–1989), she had a steamroller crush silver objects and then she hung these in 30 arrangements just above the floor. In these works, Parker transforms her damaged objects into a completely new configuration with different associations.

These are overt, physical acts of violence, but I want to explore the ways in which I and other artists do violence to the subject of our work in less obvious ways. An interviewee says:

Although I'm using reality and the visual world outside I am always wanting to change it, I realise . . . It wants to have a whole lot of other echoes to do with the imagination.

(Glover 2011)

Glover does not want simply to represent what she sees. A part of the outside visual world must be extracted and, in a sense, taken apart and reconstructed so that it encompasses the echoes of her imagination. Therefore, what is externalised through her use of her medium is not only her internal fantasy, an internal phenomenon. It is an element of the outside world transformed by her fantasy. If, as Glover states above, something in the external visual world is to be changed, its reconstruction presupposes a prior deconstruction. The 'visual world outside' has to be taken apart.

In order to make work related to Morecambe Bay, I had to appropriate my subject matter and use it ruthlessly in whatever way was necessary. I had to abstract those elements of the Bay that were essential to me for this particular work, discarding all else. When I made the piece *Under the Skin*, for instance, I was interested in the sands themselves, their movement in response to successive tides and their sinister potential to overwhelm the unwary. From early in the process, I focused on the patterns of channels in the sand and the way these were altered by each tide. Later, I chose a particular angle of shot that emphasised a threatening quality. These choices, or abstractions, were consciously made, but there was also a further process of abstraction of other elements (for instance, a certain quality of light, desaturated colours) of which I was only partially aware but which emerged in the final work. By abstracting, I was isolating my chosen elements from others that might tie the work too closely to everyday existence (for instance, a wider view of the shoreline, the inclusion of anything that would give a sense of scale or orientation). By abstracting as a means of working towards symbolisation, I was effectively breaking down my subject (the Bay), picking out some elements and discarding others.

Marion Milner discovered, in her first attempts to paint a representation of something in the outside world, that the subject of her painting remained frustratingly alien, and her attempts to paint it seemed to her to have no life. She realised that it was necessary to infuse the subject with something of her own inner life, to inhabit it imaginatively and 'spiritually envelop the object'. But she understood that this 'certainly does not preserve that thing's essential identity and nature, it rather destroys this identity in order to merge it with one's own' (Milner 1957: 57). In Milner's terms, I destroyed the identity of Morecambe Bay in order to merge it with my own. Michael Podro suggests that Milner's difficulty stemmed from a sense that the potential subject of her painting was felt by her to be already complete in itself without her intervention:

> A mode of representation that is already complete appears to the artist as alien because it is complete *despite* her. It is only by breaking down her subject matter, and that means breaking down the way it has previously been represented, that the relation to the external world can become remade for oneself, become the construction of one's own thought. This can only be done when one is sufficiently aggressive and not merely receptive.
>
> *(Podro 2007: 31)*

According to Podro, the artist's breaking down of her subject matter is a *new* breakdown of whatever aspect of the outside world the artist is responding to in her work. Podro stresses that this breaking down includes the deconstruction of previous modes of representation. The artist must find a new means of presentation, built up both from these deconstructed fragments and from aspects of her own inner life. She builds, rather than rebuilds, her subject matter in her own image, and this calls for a measure of aggression.

Dryden Goodwin speaks of taking photographs of passers-by in the street:

> *Just going back to the collection of the images on the street, you have to put yourself into a certain state because I become overwhelmed, and maybe that's important, by the kind of audacity of stealing someone's image, you know, I feel very conscious of that.*
> *(Goodwin 2011)*

As he takes the portrait photograph, he is aware that he will use it for his own purposes, deconstructing and transforming it in the process. His description of the activity as 'stealing' suggests that he recognises the inherent aggression of his action at this point. Later in this chapter, when I discuss aggression towards the medium, I refer to this artist again and to his use of an etching needle on the print during which he partially obliterates the image of the face. That is, he attacks and uses the very element of the outside world that attracted him in the first place.

All artists who respond to something in the outside world deconstruct it in order to make something new. In some cases, such as that of Cornelia Parker, the destruction is physical, but in others, such as my use of Morecambe Bay, it takes place internally. In order to create a new artwork, the artist must break down her perception of the outside world. That is, she abstracts from her perception, or her internal representation of the outside 'something', those elements that resonate with her, and she then manipulates these elements in whatever way is necessary in order to construct an artwork that will present her own personal view of this aspect of the outside world.

So far, I have discussed the artist's necessary destructiveness towards whatever aspect of the outside world she wishes to use in her artwork. This destructiveness begins with the way the artist *sees* the potential subject of her work. Her initial response involves a breaking down of her subject matter, in that she picks out elements that resonate with something in her inner world (as I described in Chapter 1) and casts the rest aside. This aspect of the artist's process can be seen as a particular instance of what Winnicott calls 'living creatively' (Winnicott 1990). Winnicott saw us all, whether artist or not, as engaged in a struggle to find personal meaning in our encounters with the outside world. To do so, we must not merely accept the world as we find it but break it down or destroy it (in fantasy) in order to create it anew for ourselves. However, for the artist, this creative apperception carries an extra charge on those occasions when it marks the beginning of a potential new work. At those moments, the artist does not only *see* the world afresh but also feels compelled to *act* – to create a new form for her experience that will eventually have an existence in the outside world. To do this, she turns to her medium.

Aggression and destructiveness appear again in the relationship between artist and medium. The sculptor Louise Bourgeois describes her process of drilling stone:

> I contemplate the penetrated cube for a long time. Then I try to express what I have to say, how I am going to translate what I have to say to it. I try to translate my problem into the stone. The drilling begins the process by negating the stone. The problem is how to complete the negation, to take away from stone, without altogether destroying it, but overcoming it, conquering it. The cube no longer exists as a pure form for contemplation; it becomes an image. I take it over with my fantasy, my life force. I put it to the use of my unconscious.
>
> *(in Stiles and Selz 2012: 40)*

There is a ruthlessness about the way Bourgeois uses the stone. She translates her problem (her 'idea') into it, and her use of the term 'translate' indicates a transfer of something from the 'language' of her idea or image (predominantly a visual language) into the haptic language of the medium. At the same time, she infuses the medium with her fantasy (a more haptic sense of her inner experience). In order to coerce the stone into becoming a form for her experience, she has to 'negate' it. Freud used the term 'negation' to refer to the repudiation, or disowning, of a previously repressed idea that has just come into consciousness (Freud 1925). Here, Bourgeois seems to be using the term to express her sense that something about *the stone* has to be repudiated. In the violent process of drilling, she repudiates the unyielding rigidity of the medium. She has somehow to make it malleable. In one sense, Bourgeois destroys the stone in one form in order to recreate it in another, but, in another sense, it must not be completely destroyed. It must retain its own particular stonelike qualities. It is through her relationship with the stone as something with its own characteristics that the new artwork will develop.

For some artists, like Bourgeois, violence towards their medium is an essential aspect of their method. The painter Howard Hodgkin explains his choice of wood rather than canvas for his painting by saying 'I want to be able to attack again and again and again, and the trouble with canvas is that if you attack it more than once or twice there's nothing left' (in Bickers and Wilson 2007: 226). The canvas is of no use to Hodgkin as it is not sufficiently resilient to withstand the aggression that is integral to his process.

Dryden Goodwin describes the way in which he attacked the 'perfect surface' of a photograph in order to create a particular work:

> *Drawings that I've made into large photographs I've taken of strangers on the streets, for example using an etching needle to inscribe into the surface of photograph, there's an interesting stage that you go through because you have a very expensive print that you ... beautifully kind of made and this surface is undefiled in any way ... When*

you make photographs you want to have a perfect surface, you want to be able to pro-tect that surface ... So by standing there and holding an etching needle in my hand, at first I feel quite self-conscious, quite ... you know there's no Apple Undo here, you know, I've got to ... I make a mark and, you know, it's there, it's permanent. So there's a dramatic tension in that.

(Goodwin 2011)

This artist has to mobilise his aggression in order to be ruthless enough to dam-age the perfect surface of his photograph. He has an intimation of the effect he wants to produce, and this can only be achieved by this violent act. Here, destructiveness is being used in the service of creativity, but nevertheless it arouses considerable anxiety. He is torn between his desire to protect the pho-tograph and the need to damage its surface, and there is a tension between these opposing impulses. He is also aware that the damage must be controlled. He must not destroy the photograph completely. It must retain something of its original character, now transformed by his actions upon it.

Another interviewee, Deborah Padfield, talks about tearing and stitching a photograph:

The photograph was of the sea and the moonlight on the sea and it's quite beautiful and I'm quite drawn, quite seduced, by that beauty but as soon as I see it I want to destroy something in it because it's not doing anything, it's not active for me ... It doesn't trigger anything beyond itself. So I think 'What is it that fascinates me about it?' So if you actually tear that area and look at that joining ... Where that process of wanting to tear and stitch it, where precisely that comes in, I think it's where destructivity and creativity are quite close. It's on that intersect. One doesn't work for me without the other ... It has to be deconstructed in some way or maybe another word for that is destroyed in some way. It has to be changed or altered so you're not looking at what you think you're looking at.

(Padfield 2011)

I want to think about what it is about this photograph that both attracts and frus-trates Padfield. The image is beautiful and seductive, and I think that her fasci-nation with it stems from the fact that it touches on something significant in her internal world. The photograph, or the original scene, appeals to her and gives rise to the intimation that she can make a new artwork. In the terms I develop in this book, it gives rise to a pre-sense. But she also knows that something needs to be done with the photograph. It is not yet 'doing anything', it is not 'active' for her. It is not yet speaking to her. She has to find a way to infuse herself into the work, and this can only be achieved by a dismantling of the photograph. She chooses to do this by the process of tearing and re-stitching.

The instances I have discussed above all involve a violent process that is integral to the artist's practice. But violence can also come in as a response to a situation that occurs while the artist is working with her medium. The painter

Estelle Thompson says 'when I say reworked it can mean that the whole thing literally gets sanded back. At times I've even used paint stripper and become quite abusive in the sanding of a surface' (Thompson 2017). This interviewee is talking about the situation in which she discovers that a painting that she has been working on for some time does not yet feel right. Her use of the word 'abusive' emphasises the ruthlessness of her attack on her medium. She feels compelled to do whatever is necessary to get rid of the part of the painting that is not working for her.

Joyce McDougall writes of the struggle between the artist and her medium in which the artist both enters states of union with her medium and attacks it:

> Thus the medium … will always present itself as both an ally and an enemy. The medium of creative expression has to be 'tamed' so that the creator can impose his or her will upon it; it must translate the creator's inner vision, sometimes evoking a transcendent feeling of union with it.
>
> *(McDougall 1995: 58)*

I want to take McDougall's use of the word 'tame' here and suggest that the artist must *both* tame the medium *and* allow it not to be tamed. That is, if she has a particular idea or image of the work she wants to create, she will try to impose her will on the medium, will try to 'tame' it, but it is the medium's refusal to be tamed, its assertion of its own qualities, that sets up a potential space between artist and medium from which a new form, embodying an aspect of the artist's inner world, may emerge.

McDougall bases her writing about the creative process on her psychoanalytic work with artists, writers and scientists who came to her as patients, often seeking analysis because of blocks in their process. From her experience with these patients, and from her reading of Klein, she induces that '*violence is an essential element* in all creative production' (McDougall 1995: 55, italics in original). She quotes a painter who had been in analysis as writing:

> The profound primordial drives that surge up in me can become powerful enough to cause discomfort; the constant build up of tension has to be put outside me into the outer world in order to restore some feeling of harmony inside. It is creation, but it is fired by feelings of destruction. When I cannot paint, I become the target of my own violent aggression.
>
> *(ibid.: 56)*

For this artist, the making of art is an expression of destructive drives that need to be externalised. Indeed, McDougall writes that 'we might envisage the internal world of the creative person as something like a volcano' (1995: 249). This image epitomises McDougall's view of the creative process as intrinsically violent, rooted in libidinal drives. However, McDougall is writing from her perspective as a psychoanalyst working with patients who are artists, whereas my own research is based on interviews with artists who are not (necessarily) in analysis. Judging from the evidence of the artist interviews, McDougall's image of a volcanic internal world is not universally applicable to all artists, but her statement that the artwork 'must translate the creator's inner vision' and her emphasis on the centrality of violence are in accord with my own findings.

McDougall was influenced by several psychoanalytic schools, including the Kleinians. The Kleinian view of the artist's process is that the creation of an artwork provides the artist with a means of repairing a damaged internal object (this is discussed in more detail in Chapter 4). Adrian Stokes, writing from a Kleinian viewpoint, sees the reparative potential of art-making as dependent upon a prior destructiveness towards the artist's medium. That is, he sees the artist as not only repairing the damage done (in phantasy) towards an internal object but also re-enacting that damage, now in relation to the medium. He links this to his own concepts of carving and modelling:

> I turn now to the major overall process, reparation, in which both the good breast and the whole, independent mother must figure, a reparation dependent, it seems to me, upon initial attack. I believe that in the creation of art there exists a preliminary element of acting out of aggression, an acting out that then accompanies reparative transformation, by which inequalities, tension and distortions, for instance, are integrated, are made to 'work'. I have long held the distinction between carving and modeling to be generic in an application to all the visual arts. These two activities have many differences from the psychological angle, first, I think, in the degree and quality of the attack upon the material … A painter, then, to be so, must be capable of perpetrating defacement; though it be defacement in order to add, create, transform, restore, the attack is defacement nonetheless.
>
> *(Stokes 2014: 74–75)*

According to this reading, the destructive aspect of Padfield's attacks on the photograph seem to have a dual function. They both re-enact the original phantasised attack and contribute to its repair through the making of the finished work. On one level, a Kleinian reading seems to fit the facts of many artistic productions, particularly those involving overt acts of destruction such as Padfield's photograph or Cornelia's Parker's *30 Pieces of Silver* and *Cold Dark Matter: An Exploded View* described at the beginning of this chapter. But it seems to me that the full picture may be more complex. The findings of the research underpinning this book suggest that the view that the prime function of making art is to put right a phantasised act of destruction that has already happened is too restrictive. Although the interviews can never uncover the unconscious motivations driving an artist, they point towards a wide variety of internal experiences and suggest that the inner something that has given rise to the artist's pre-sense *may or may not* be related to a phantasy of inner damage. That is, the concept of the pre-sense relates to something as-yet unformed in the artist's inner experience but does not restrict this to the phantasy of damage done to an internal object.

The psychoanalyst Ken Robinson makes an important point when he says:

> One strand of theory sees creativity as a making good but I am suggesting that although creative vitality might well on occasion be offered repara-tively, out of love, concern and self-preservation, it is important not to confuse how it is *used* with its ontology. Reparation is not the motor of creativity.
>
> *(Robinson 2017)*

Robinson, following Winnicott, sees creativity as the continuation of a process that begins in the relationship between mother and infant. It is essential to our sense of being alive. Here, I am saying that the way in which each artist *uses* cre-ativity is not confined to reparation but differs according to his or her particular internal experiences.

The Kleinian emphasis on repair also seems at odds with the artist's own sense that the value of her work lies in its newness, that it is a form that has never existed before. Marion Milner emphasises this newness, writing:

> For the artist as artist, rather than as patient, and for whoever responds to his work, I think that the essential point is the new thing he has created, the new bit of the external world that he has made significant and 'real' through endowing it with form.
>
> *(Milner 1957: 160)*

Here, Milner seems to be using the term 'real' to denote the external existence of the artwork, its existence in its own right rather than as a substitute for some-thing else. Milner also has a different approach to the question of destructiveness. She does not write directly about aggression towards her medium, although she does refer to many instances of aggression and destructiveness in the content of her paintings. However, I find her description of her psychoanalytic work with an 11-year-old boy (Milner 1952a) to be relevant here. I referred to this paper in Chapter 5 where I discussed the boy's use of Milner as a pliable medium. Here, I want to focus on the destructive aspects of his play with her. Milner writes of the boy's use of her in a complex drama enacted through his play with toys and other materials in the consulting room. The drama, which included destructive acts such as setting objects on fire, was directed by the boy and Milner was required to play a series of parts. She describes the way in which she allowed him to use her as if she were a persecuted schoolboy: 'I was set long monotonous tasks, my efforts were treated with scorn, I was forbidden to talk and made to write out 'lines' if I did; and if I did not comply with these demands, then he wanted to cane me' (ibid.: 91). And, of his general behaviour towards her, she writes: 'He so often treated me as totally his own to do what he liked with, as though I were dirt, his dirt, or as a tool, an extension of his own hand' (ibid.: 94). Milner's analytic work with this boy could only progress through her willingness to act as his medium, and this included her willingness to allow his destructive acts directed towards her. She came to understand that, through his play, in which he treated her as a character in his inner drama, he was gradually able to relate to her as a person in her own right in the external world:

> It seemed as if it was only by being able, again and again, to experience the illusion that I was part of himself, fused with the goodness that he could conceive of internally, that he became able to tolerate a goodness that was not his own creation and to allow me goodness independently ... The repeated discovery that I went on being friendly, and remained unhurt by him, in spite of the continual attacks on me, certainly played a very important part.
>
> *(Milner 1952a: 103–104)*

Michael Parsons compares the boy's relationship with Milner to the artist's relationship with her medium:

> The boy used her as a pliable medium that he could mould however he wanted except that she also had qualities of her own to be taken account of. So his being able to make things out of his pliable medium depended also on his discovering things about it at the same time. The artist has just such a relation to his or her artistic medium. The mixed process of invention and discovery is the same.
>
> *(Parsons 2000: 162)*

It was necessary for the boy to be able to use Milner in whatever way he wanted, as if she were part of himself, in order to discover her and himself as separate beings. In a parallel way, the artist uses her medium, feels free to attack it and, in doing so, discovers its own properties and behaviour. Out of this interaction a new work with a life of its own may emerge.

I want to take up Parson's discussion of the boy's use of Milner to argue that the relationship between artist and medium can be compared to the patient's use of the analyst more generally. The artist interacts with her medium, nudging or coercing it into a form that mirrors her experience. Sometimes, the medium responds predictably, following the artist's sense of what she wants it to do. But at other times, it behaves in unexpected ways, frustrating the artist's intended actions upon it. At such moments, the artist may find another way to follow her idea, or she may welcome the new direction suggested by the medium's behaviour. In a similar way, the patient tries to recruit the analyst to play a particular role, to reflect her experience. But the analyst will sometimes resist this coercion and, perhaps, offer an unexpected interpretation. The psychoanalyst Joseph Sandler wrote about this in his paper 'Counter-transference and Role-responsiveness' (1976). He argues that the patient 'nudges' the analyst to behave in certain ways in relation to him. The patient, according to Sandler, casts him- or herself in a particular role and puts pressure on the analyst to play out a complementary role. Initially, the analyst may unconsciously comply until some incident clarifies what is happening. At this point, the analyst is able to change his or her behaviour and the meaning of the incident can be explored. Such moments may prove to be turning points in the course of an analysis. In an analogous way, an artist may coerce her medium to behave in a particular way, but it may sometimes frustrate her expectations and behave differently. This may lead the artist in an unexpected and fruitful new direction.

Above, I have discussed the artist's aggression towards her medium. I want now to differentiate the medium from the developing artwork in order to distinguish between two situations. The first is that in which the artist is pursuing an idea and finds that she must act aggressively or destructively towards her *medium* to make it comply with her wishes. I have discussed this above. The second situation is that in which the artist finds that the developing artwork does not feel 'right'. I write about my own stormy relationship with a developing artwork:

> There were times when I felt frustrated with the medium I was using because I couldn't make it produce anything that fitted the idea in my head. Although that seems to imply that I had a clear idea in my head, which, most of the time, I did not. It was a sort of love/hate relationship with the artwork as it developed. There were moments when I was involved with it in an excited way and other times when I wanted to destroy it.

Here, I am referring both to my frustration with my medium for not allowing me to follow my idea but also to my frustration with the developing artwork. The developing artwork was a manifestation of my idea, but I sometimes felt it was unsatisfactory because it was not a sufficiently close reflection of my pre-sense. At those moments, I wanted to destroy it. This sometimes led me to discard a particular set of images or abandon a particular approach in order to find something more satisfying, something that would fit my pre-sense more closely. This was part and parcel of my process but nevertheless called for a willingness to destroy or discard something that I had valued. In Chapter 5, I discussed the first incarnation of the developing artwork that eventually became *The Transience of Wonder*. I was not satisfied with the form of the work as a large photographic print (Figure 5.1), although at the time I could not see why this was or how I could develop it further. I thought at that point that the indexical nature of the work was key in that each 'slice' of sky was related to a particular moment in time and a particular spatial point. I went on to change the configuration of the 'slices' to emphasise this aspect more clearly (I discuss this more fully in Chapter 10), but the resulting form still did not feel 'right'. Eventually, after much trial and error, I decided to abandon this approach entirely. In order to find a new way forward, I had to reject much of the work I had already done.

In this case, it was not primarily the medium but the *developing artwork* that frustrated me. It did not seem to me to correspond sufficiently closely with my pre-sense. I could not recognise myself in the work. The initial idea now seemed not quite right after all, and I realised that there had to be a shift in the idea that might call for a renewed attack on the medium.

A photographer describes the need for a ruthless edit when a particular combination of images does not feel right:

> *I've learned you've got to get rid of your favourite quite often. In fact you have to get rid of them... You have to realise that they don't work . . . I suppose it's like a pruning. You've got a bush that you like and you have got to chop off a bit that's not working, even if it's a lovely bush.*
>
> *(Bonnell 2011)*

In this case, it is not entirely evident whether the artist's aggression is primarily directed towards the developing artwork or towards the medium. If it is towards her medium, she continues to pursue her first idea, but some of the images do not fit with it and so must be given up. On the other hand, it may be that her aggression is directed primarily towards the developing artwork as she realises that a particular idea for the final artwork is no longer working. Her resulting *aggression towards her developing artwork* leads to a change in the idea, resulting in the need to eliminate certain images, even if they are her favourites. In that case, aggression towards the medium would be secondary.

If the artist finds that the developing artwork no longer 'feels right', she may encounter a dead end that calls for the eradication of part (or all) of the work and a return to an earlier stage. Jon Thomson, who works with Alison Craighead, says:

> *Sometimes we'll be working on things and we'll push it to a certain point – perhaps put quite a lot of work into it – and then we'll realise that the best thing we can possibly do is to take it all apart and begin again, or strip it back or just take the one thing ... Over the years we have had to learn to be quite brutal about cutting stuff away, getting rid of it – things that might be good in and of themselves but it doesn't work in terms of the piece of work you are trying to make.*
>
> *(Thomson and Craighead 2011)*

Thomson's language emphasises the violence of what needs to be done. He and his partner have to be 'brutal', to 'cut stuff away'. Like Bonnell above, they must avoid being seduced by some element that might be good in itself.

For a painter, this return to an earlier stage may mean removing the paint already applied: 'Everything grinds to a halt and it's really frustrating and it might be that you really have to scrape it back to almost nothing to resolve it' (Henrietta Simson). I discussed the incubation of an idea for a new work in

Chapter 2, but it is also relevant here. The 'scraping back to almost nothing' may call for a period of gestation before a new way forward can be found.

This point of frustration and the mobilising of aggression necessary to get rid of that part of the developing artwork that is 'not working' may be an important step in the making of a satisfying work. Simson continues: 'Some paintings might happen without that brick wall that you have to face at some point and they make me more anxious than the other ones because I think they've been too easy. They've come too easy in a way' (2011). This artist insists that, for a work to be satisfying, there must be a problem to be overcome. If, as I argue, the making of an artwork is a search for a form for something that was previously formless, this raises the question of whether, if the form comes too easily, it may have already been 'known' by the artist at a level below conscious awareness. She is looking for something in herself that is not yet known. As another interviewee says: 'I wouldn't start it if I knew what it was going to be . . . So I only want to make something that I don't know what it's going to be' (John Aiken).

The painter Frank Auerbach continually scrapes off the day's paint and begins again the next day:

> I just scrape it down because that's the way I work. Because I can't get the living entity unless everything in the picture is in reaction to everything else... In my case what you see on the canvas is the result of the last bout, almost entirely.
>
> *(in Peppiat 2012: 11)*

Auerbach feels compelled to repaint until something happens within the painting that makes him feel that he has captured 'the living entity'. Through his process of continually destroying and remaking his work, he eventually succeeds in getting something of himself into it and, when he does so, it takes on this new life.

In order to bring her work to life, every artist must find a way to imbue it with some aspect of her own inner experience, and this does not happen automatically. The artist must find a way to inject or force herself into the developing work, and this inevitably involves aggression and ruthlessness. Perhaps this is why Winnicott wrote:

> The creative artist or thinker may, in fact, fail to understand, or even may despise, the feelings of concern that motivate a less creative person; and of artists it may be said that some have no capacity for guilt and yet achieve a socialization through their exceptional talent. Ordinary guilt-ridden people find this bewildering; yet they have a sneaking regard for ruthlessness that does in fact, in such circumstances, achieve more than guilt-driven labour.
>
> *(Winnicott 1958: 26)*

Winnicott seems to imply that artists are less guilt-ridden than other people, but I would put it differently. The making of art may well arouse feelings of guilt, but the artist has to overcome these feelings sufficiently to be able to exercise the ruthlessness necessary for her work to proceed. It is not that there is no capacity for guilt but, rather, that the compulsion to make the work is so strong that guilt cannot be allowed to halt the process.

8

SPACES AND FRAMES

I need to create boundaries – they [routines] are kind of boundaries, aren't they? ... I think they calm me down.

Jo Volley

The painter Tomma Abts consistently uses a format of 48 by 36 centimetres for her paintings. She says:

> At some point I decided on that size. It felt right. I think it relates to the size of a head space. The vertical format holds the space tight. A landscape format would let the tension flow out on the sides.
>
> *(Abts 2013: 58)*

It is clear from Abts' description that the physical frame of her paintings acts as a container, keeping the energy of the image packed tightly into the limited space. She did not decide on this format before she began her series of paintings, however. Rather, the choice was made 'at some point' when her process had progressed to the degree that she knew 'it felt right'. Once she had made this decision, subsequent paintings all started with this pre-determined frame.

The frame of the artwork contains the work not only physically but also psychically, in the sense that it must hold that aspect of the artist's inner experience that is given form. This experience is an emotional one and can include intense feelings, either positive or negative, that may be difficult to bear. A vivid example of this is the work of Louise Bourgeois, whose own writings (2012) reveal that she used her experience of psychoanalysis not to 'cure' herself of her symptoms but to intensify them so that she could put them into her artworks. The psychoanalyst Juliet Mitchell writes: 'It is not just that Bourgeois makes real and concrete what she feels and experiences, it is that she goes into what is unbearable/ unknowable (which is why it is repressed) and makes it conscious in visual form' (Mitchell 2012: 51). Bourgeois' artworks act as containers for her unbearable experiences of hatred, destructiveness and jealousy, and these experiences are 'forced' into the works. In the face of such violence, the work itself must be strong enough to withstand the pressure of its contents.

From her own experience of painting, Marion Milner wrote about the empty space of the blank canvas as a frame and suggested that this space was a necessary prerequisite of her art. She went on to write that the frame 'marks off an area within which what is perceived has to be taken symbolically, while what is outside the frame is taken literally' (Milner 1957: 158). By 'literally', Milner means that what is outside the frame is to be regarded as part of the world of external, shared 'reality'. The frame here can be understood in a wide sense to include not only the frame of a two-dimensional work but also the frame of the screen, the edges of a sculptural object or installation and the temporal limits of a play or film. Winnicott writes: 'One example of … unthinkable anxiety is the state in which there is no frame to the picture; nothing to contain the interweaving of forces in the inner psychic reality, and in practical terms no-one to hold the baby' (Winnicott 1989: 115). Although Winnicott is referring to psychosomatic disorders rather than art and his 'frame to the picture' is a metaphorical one, his comment links with Milner's interest in the physical frame of a painting, and he draws a direct parallel between the holding function of the frame and that of the mother.

The frame of any specific work is determined by a series of decisions in which the artist gradually narrows down the available options. Hughie O'Donoghue says: 'before you make your next painting or your next work, everything in the world is possible theoretically, so it's a process of elimination'. This process can be understood as comprising several phases. First, the artist decides on her medium. Some artists use a range of media and so choose a particular one (or more than one) for each work or series of works. Others make a once-and-for-all decision to concentrate on a particular field:

> I'd decided I wanted to be a painter but there were lots of people encouraging me to do other things … but I thought I'm going to persevere with painting. So … I've narrowed things down, I'm not going to go off doing this or doing that … I'm going to try and develop my vision as a painter.
>
> (O'Donoghue 2013)

Having made the decision to work within a particular medium, a second stage follows in which the artist chooses a particular methodology and range of interests. This choice will be influenced by her personal concerns, her inner world, as well as aesthetic preferences and the desire to work within, or react against, particular artistic movements (themselves another kind of frame). The choice is likely to affect the artist's entire oeuvre, or, at least, a series of works, rather than a single piece:

I'm going to make a painting and it's then about the particular kind of painting. And my painting is particularly about... awareness of paint as a natural stuff, a substance ... whether it's a painting of, you know, a man lying in a field, it's also just paint and colour ... there's that kind of self-conscious awareness of what it physically is ... that's always at the forefront of my mind.

(ibid.)

In addition to these choices, each of which narrows the available options and so frames the final work more closely, the artist decides on the form and dimensions of a particular work, its physical frame:

That's part of my creative process actually, deciding how thick the wood is going to be that the canvas sits on, how many openings at the back of the stretcher there are going to be ... those sorts of decisions are quite particular, and they contribute to the success or not of the painting. Once you've made a decision that you're making a canvas, it's eight feet by seven feet ... it's just one thing that's become fixed.

(ibid.)

Painters usually need to make decisions about the size of the canvas or board, the physical frame of the work, before they begin work. Artists in other media may make equivalent decisions at later stages. For instance, a sculptor may decide on the form and dimensions of the final work some way into her process, whilst a photographer may choose the size of her prints in relation only to a particular exhibition.

Decisions at each of the above stages narrow the options open to the artist and so provide a metaphorical as well as a physical frame. The artist may feel contained by the limits each decision imposes. But there is also a danger that any decision may be over-restricting, imposing too great a restraint on the artist. Sometimes a particular framing decision may need to be reversed or revised. This is easier in some media than others, but even painters need the flexibility to modify their decisions if the work demands it. As O'Donoghue says: 'you can cut it down, you can add a bit onto the side which I've done over the years, I've changed things'.

The artist Martin Creed claims that at the beginning of creating a new work everything is possible, but whilst O'Donoghue sees his process as gradually narrowing down the possibilities, Creed sees himself as trying to keep his options open. He wants to avoid setting limits: 'I don't want to choose because I don't know what to choose.' Rather, he wants to keep possibilities open:

In the microcosm of a work you can have everything. So on a piano you can play every note or, you know ... if you make a microcosm you can, you can, you can make your own wee world where you can have everything. I mean along certain lines.

(Caldwell and Creed 2012)

This statement is reminiscent of Ehrenzweig's concept of dedifferentiation when he writes: 'What is common to all examples of dedifferentiation is their freedom from having to make a choice' (Ehrenzweig 1967: 32). According to Ehrenzweig, dedifferentiation is an essential stage on the way to making a new work. But for Ehrenzweig, it is a stage, not the end condition. From Creed's statement, it seems that he wants to remain in a state of dedifferentiation in relation to his work, to avoid making choices that would tie it down. Psychoanalyst Lesley Caldwell links this desire to 'have it all, all the time' to the qualities of the unconscious described by Freud and suggests that perhaps, in his work, Creed addresses the question of what art is and how it differs (if at all) from other activities in life. However, despite his assertion that he can have everything, Creed himself qualifies this by adding 'along certain lines'. In fact, Creed is obliged to make choices in order to complete a work. As just one example, in *Work no. 850* (2008), for which runners sprinted through the Duveen Gallery at Tate Britain, Creed chose the speed of the running, the interval between runners and so on. Whether he wishes it or not, these decisions delimit his work. I argue that the artist cannot completely avoid the fact that the creation of an artwork involves moving on from the state of dedifferentiation to a more delineated form.

A further frame is provided by the setting in which the finished work is exhibited. The 'framed gap' of the Duveen Gallery provides a boundaried setting that contains Creed's performance. If the artist develops her artwork with a particular space in mind then this provides both limits and possibilities for the work in hand. As Sharon Kivland says: 'That may come right at the beginning – the thinking how... that may be built into it. Because how it's displayed produces the way that it looks. But not for all works.' For some works, such as installation pieces, her knowledge of the exhibition space has a crucial effect upon the development of the work. For others, the work may be developed without reference to a particular space. When I developed my video work *Under the Skin*, at the beginning of the process I did not have a specific exhibition space in mind. The work was intended for projection, but this could be achieved in a variety of venues. Later, as the work neared completion, I decided that I wanted to show it as a rear projection in a doorway. I hoped that the viewer would have the impression of a room full of sand moving strangely, and that this might induce an anxiety that the sand would flood out at any moment. This effect could not be created by a projection onto a wall. Having been offered a venue with a suitable doorway (the entrance hall of Ruskin's house, Brantwood), there was a further stage of development as I adjusted the dimensions of the work to fit the space (literally a framed gap), researched suitable projectors and screens, and made many decisions about the final appearance of the work in this particular setting (see Figure 8.1).

Considering the framing of *Under the Skin*, in one sense the frame of the doorway separated the space outside the frame from that inside it. Following Milner's argument (Milner 1952b), what was seen within the space inside the door frame was to be regarded in a different way from the space of the room outside the

FIGURE 8.1 *Under the Skin.* HD video animation. Brantwood, Coniston, 2013

frame. The room belonged to everyday life whilst the work, within the door frame, was to be received as a symbolic presentation. But, for this installation, the situation was not as clear-cut as this. The impact of the work did not reside only in the moving image within the door frame. It relied on the fact that this was situated within a domestic environment. The threatening sand appeared as if it were in the adjoining room, as if the frame of the door might not be sufficient to contain it. So the door frame became part of the work itself, and it could be argued that the whole domestic setting was intrinsic to its effect. That is, the boundaries of the work became fluid, reflecting the fact that it was concerned with exploring a sense of the uncontainable.

The painter Imran Qureshi both embraces and subverts the containing function of the frame in his installation *Where the Shadows Are So Deep* (Qureshi 2016). This work comprises a series of exquisite miniatures depicting trees with anthropomorphic qualities as they lean towards each other, lie uprooted or communicate through intertwining tendrils. Serene in the first images, contained within the miniature's traditional multiple borders, the trees become increasingly fragmented and frenetic. As they do so, violations of the frame gradually appear. The image slips to one side as if trying to escape; bloody marks appear within it; the white border is besmirched with dabs of paint; the frame sometimes disappears altogether. The image itself, no longer protected by an inviolable border, becomes unstable. The meticulously ordered universe of the miniature begins to break down. At the same time, the floor and walls of the gallery are splashed with sprawling blood-red paintings as if this were the scene of a recent atrocity.

Qureshi disrupts the strict rules of miniature paintings, allowing his images to leak out of their containing frames, creating a powerful impression of a loss of law and order and an outbreak of violence.

In Qureshi's work, and in my own installation of *Under the Skin*, the subversion of frames becomes part of the work, but this does not negate the existence of a containing space for the work as a whole. For Qureshi's *Where the Shadows Are So Deep*, the gallery space (the Barbican Curve) provided this. For *Under the Skin*, similarly, the entrance hall in which the piece was shown acted as a container, although the question of which elements of that space could also be regarded as part of the work remained fluid.

Having considered the frame of the artwork and the spaces, such as the gallery, that may contain it, I want to go on to think about the space the artist herself inhabits as she creates the work. The studio, a physical space set apart from everyday life and dedicated to the making of art, is the prototypical workspace of the artist and each artist who works from a studio sets up her own idiosyncratic environment there. Henry Moore collected pieces of driftwood and other items and kept them in his studio, where they inspired him in relation to new works. By contrast, Tomma Abts works in a bare room, windowless except for a skylight. Anthony Cragg says his studio is 'a kind of playground for myself that allows me a relatively free association with the material' (in Goertz 2016). His 'playground' is a boundaried space that contains all the materials he needs and that allows him the mental space to respond imaginatively, playfully, to those materials. The studio offers containment through physical boundaries, and the possibility of temporal ones too in that the artist may decide to spend certain periods of time in this space.

The artist Shirazeh Houshiary speaks of the importance of the studio for her: 'When you're in the outside world, you are busy with domestic or everyday events. Here you leave all that behind; it's a place where you are free, without any involvement with the outside world . . . a place to let go' (in Amirsadeghi and Homayoun Eisler 2012: 54). Houshiary speaks of a particular kind of freedom, the freedom to cast aside the constraints of everyday life and to follow one's own path. Possible disturbances are, as far as possible, removed. One of the interviewees, Nina Rodin, describes how she tries to achieve this:

> *I am building a new studio. There is almost a sense of nesting: both removing extraneous stuff and being specific about what is needed. I have painted the floor grey. . . . I needed it to become neutral space where things could happen. The studio walls are white because I don't want distractions.*
>
> *(Rodin 2011)*

This artist's comparison of her studio to a nest evokes a sense of safety and containment in a carefully prepared protective space. The potential disturbances the artist wants to guard against are not only ones from outside that might threaten the external frame but also ones from within herself. The bare floor and walls will help her to remain focused on her work.

Winnicott writes about the importance of the mother's ability to provide a contained space, protected from outside impingements, within which the infant's development can progress. He calls this space the 'facilitating environment' (Winnicott 1963c). According to Winnicott, the mother has two roles in relation to her child – a role as an object to whom the child can relate and a role as provider of an environment that will foster development:

> it seems possible to use these words 'object mother' and 'environment mother' … to describe the vast difference that there is for the infant between two aspects of infant-care, the mother as object, or owner of the part-object that may satisfy the infant's urgent needs, and the mother as the person who wards off the unpredictable and who actively provides care in handling and in general management.
>
> *(Winnicott 1963b: 74)*

The facilitating environment is a safe space within which the infant can develop, but this very development is predicated on the infant's changing relationship with the 'mother as object'. That is, the infant needs a contained setting for his relationship with his mother and the mother herself provides this. In a parallel way, the artist needs a contained setting for the ongoing relationship between her and her artwork. However, the artist must provide this environment for herself and the studio is one means of doing so.

The artist's studio can be compared to the psychoanalyst's consulting room in that both offer a contained space, protected from interruptions, within which specialised work can take place. Just as the artist needs certain conditions in order to enter the state of mind necessary for her creative process, the patient in analysis needs the analyst to provide a containing space, a 'facilitating environment', within which she can engage in the analysis. The psychoanalyst Andrea Sabbadini compares the analyst's consulting room to the artist's studio, writing that within the 'consistent and therefore relatively safe space provided by our "studios"' (Sabbadini 2013: 120) the analyst can make creative use of the material brought by the patient.

The facilitating environment provided by the psychoanalyst does not only consist in the physical environment of the consulting room. In addition, the prescribed duration of the analytic session, the analytic 'rules' and the professionalism of the analyst act together to give the patient a sense of containment. There are also parallels here with the artist's situation. Temporal boundaries provide another type of external frame for the artist. She decides how long she will spend in her studio or other workspace, and at the end of that period she knows she will emerge again into everyday life:

> *I do get into quite an intense state, I think, where the brain sort of slips into something else… But I think if I went on like that without seeing… other people then the work wouldn't work because I would have tipped over the edge.*
>
> *(Padfield 2011)*

Because Padfield knows that, at a certain point, she will stop work, see other people and return to everyday concerns, she feels safe enough to allow herself to enter her working state of mind. Similarly, in a psychoanalytic session the patient's knowledge that, at the end of the analytic 'hour', she will return to her everyday life can enable her to enter a different state of mind for the duration of the session.

Spatial and temporal boundaries can be considered as external factors that contribute to the artist's sense of containment. I will call these factors the artist's 'external frame'. The external frame may include procedural boundaries in addition to spatial and temporal ones. For instance, one of the interviewees works by deciding in advance upon a set of processes that she then follows in order to make the work. She compares her process to a scientific procedure in which she follows her protocol in order to discover what the result might be. This procedure gives her a sense of freedom within the limits she has set herself:

> *I wonder whether sometimes I set up those processes or protocols so that I can then just be able to enjoy the painting for what it is… Perhaps having set up that protocol, I am then quite free to paint each one of these layers, and be free in what they could be and in what I put in the layers because I do not have to justify each image as it appears. The protocol does that. So there is the possibility of emotion in there but it doesn't halt the process, it doesn't matter if I don't like it.*
>
> *(Rodin 2011)*

Rodin spoke elsewhere in her interview of her 'overpowering yearning' to paint. Her protocols create a frame within which she can enjoy the painting without being overwhelmed by a powerful emotional response to her work. By 'justifying each image as it appears', she seems to be referring to the experience of painting without her protocol when she feels that 'each brushstroke is a decision' and she fears that her emotional response to the developing work might be strong enough to stop her in her tracks. The structure of the protocol seems not only to provide containment but is also something to hold on to in the maelstrom of her responses.

The artist and writer Rebecca Fortnum has interviewed women artists about their working practices (Fortnum 2007). She describes the total engagement of the artist at work as 'living in' the artwork and discusses the way in which each artist creates the conditions for this state of mind by putting boundaries in place. In her interview with Fortnum, artist Vanessa Jackson says: 'I'm happy with the notion of rules because we all have rules and we spend an inordinate amount of time being in them and then trying to break them … The rules are to set up a space that I can dwell in' (ibid.: 139). The rules, whether they are adhered to or not, provide an enabling structure and make it possible for the artist to enter her working state of mind.

Returning to the parallel between the containing space provided for the patient by the analyst and that provided by the artist for herself, the above quotation highlights an important difference between the two situations. The analyst, like the artist, puts procedural boundaries in place. In psychoanalysis, these include the analytic 'rules' of the analyst's professional behaviour and the 'rules' with which the patient is expected to comply (such as timekeeping, contact between sessions, payment, etc.). But the artist must guard against the possibility that her self-imposed rules might become too restricting. Jackson emphasises the fact that the rules are there both to contain and to be pushed against. For the artist, breaking rules may be an important part of the process. For the psychoanalyst, adherence to the rules of professional behaviour is essential (although the *patient's* pushing against the rules may be part of the analytic work).

Whether or not she has a studio or sets up particular procedural 'rules', each artist finds her own way to create a bounded 'external frame' within which she can work. The function of these boundaries is to establish the conditions for the artist to enter a different *internal* space. An interviewee says: 'The spaces are important. I obviously need space to work in and I need that psychological space to be free to explore and make mistakes – to allow failure' (Mills 2011). In the next chapter, I consider the nature of this psychological or internal space.

9

THE ARTIST'S INTERNAL FRAME

It's what I call shed mentality. . . . a laboratory of the mind.

Russell Mills

The artist Shezad Dawood, speaking of the location of creative thought, describes 'a kind of inner mansion where you have a number of connecting rooms' (in Amirsadeghi and Homayoun Eisler 2012: 40), whilst Grayson Perry says:

> My own creativity and art practice has been a mental shed – a sanctuary as well as a place of action – where I have retreated to make things. It gives me a sense of security in a safe, enclosed space while I look out the window to the world.
>
> *(Jones and Perry 2007: 23)*

Perry's 'mental shed' takes on the characteristics of the shed that his father used as a workshop, whilst Dawood's has grander proportions. Speaking of the internal spaces of the imagination, Dawood, Perry and Mills use the metaphor of rooms, envisaging the internal equivalent of a physical outside space. I will call this internal space the artist's 'internal frame'.

In the last chapter, I considered the various ways in which the artist constructs a containing space, framed physically, temporally and procedurally. Now I want to think about the way in which this 'external frame' sets the scene for a movement into an 'internal frame' within which the artist can be in her working state of mind. In Chapter 5, I quoted an interviewee as saying:

> *In the studio I have to be in a certain state . . . it's about being very involved. What's very schematic, very structural in its approach is then set aside as you become involved in that pocket you've created to lose yourself in the activity.*
>
> *(Goodwin 2011)*

Here, I want to consider what this artist means by a 'pocket'. In everyday language, a pocket is a small containing space within a larger garment or bag, and I think that here Goodwin is talking about an internal containing space, facilitated by the external space of his studio. Once he is in this 'pocket', a space he himself has created for the purpose, he feels able to 'lose' himself in his work.

Marion Milner, writing about losing oneself in an activity, refers to the need for a 'safe setting, a setting that will still be there when one emerges again into ordinary self-awareness' (Milner 1952b: 81). Milner uses the term 'reverie' for the state of mind of the artist while working. She writes:

> For the word 'reverie' does emphasise the aspect of absentmindedness, and therefore brings in what I feel to be a very important aspect of the problem, that is, the necessity for a certain quality of protectiveness in the environment. For there are obviously many circumstances in which it is not safe to be absent-minded; it needs a setting, both physical and mental. It requires a physical setting in which we are freed, for the time being, from the need for immediate practical expedient action; and it requires a mental setting, an attitude, both in the people around and in oneself, a tolerance of something which at moments looks very like madness.
>
> *(Milner 1957: 163–164)*

According to Milner's formulation, the necessary physical and mental settings are closely bound up with each other, and their essential function is to protect the artist while she is in an absent-minded state, the state she calls reverie. I am interpreting Milner's 'absent-mindedness' as a state of being absent from the concerns of everyday life. The artist is anything but absent from the concerns relating to her developing artwork, as I discussed in earlier chapters. Milner compares this state to 'madness', by which I understand her to mean that the temporary relaxing of boundaries between the artist and the developing artwork has something in common with psychotic states in which differentiation between inner and outer worlds breaks down. In the terms I introduce in this book, this refers to moments when the artist's 'extended self' holds sway. Milner qualifies her comparison by saying that the mental state only looks like madness to other people. To the artist herself it does not. This is because the artist retains some connection with the outer world through her 'observer' mode of functioning. However, the artist may sometimes fear that her state of mind could tip into madness, that she might lose touch with her 'observer self'.

In the quotation above, Milner points out that the necessary setting is both physical and mental. I have discussed the physical setting in Chapter 8, and now I want to consider the mental one. Milner writes:

> Then I came back to the role of the will, how in painting it seems to come in through restricting one's attention to the blank space to be filled together with the model, still life, landscape or whatever, and one's own

feelings about this. The will making a kind of frame for what I have come to call contemplative action.

(Milner 1952b: 81)

Here, Milner's 'will' seems to refer to an effort of concentration, a refusal of distractions. The resulting 'frame' must be an internal psychic one, and it seems to relate to the 'mental setting' she mentions above (although in the previous quotation Milner represents the 'mental setting' as a tolerance of the artist's state of mind, whereas here she emphasises the limitation of the artist's attention to the task in hand). At this point, I want to take up the idea of the 'mental setting' as an internal psychic space or, to use the terminology of Dryden Goodwin from the beginning of this chapter, a 'pocket'.

I want to differentiate here between the artist's *state* of mind and her *frame* of mind. I introduce the concept of the artist's 'internal frame of mind' to refer to an internal containing structure that holds the artist mentally and allows her to feel sufficiently safe to enter and remain in her working *state* of mind. This internal frame, according to my definition, is a psychic space within which the artist feels free to listen to her own responses to her developing artwork. It is a space for the artwork within the artist's mind where unconscious symbolic meaning holds sway.

The artist's internal frame parallels the psychoanalyst's internal analytic setting as proposed by Michael Parsons:

The analytic setting exists not only externally but also internally as a structure in the mind of the analyst. The internal analytic setting constitutes an area of the analyst's mind where reality is defined by unconscious symbolic meaning. . . . The internal setting can help analysts listen inwardly to themselves in a way that is free-floating with regard to their internal processes.

(Parsons 2007: 1441)

Parsons points out that each patient affects the analyst in particular ways, including ways that have to do with work that the analyst still needs to do on herself. Her internal psychoanalytic setting allows her to feel safe enough to recognise these affects and to use them both to help the patient and to work on herself. Just as the analyst at work is listening for the inherent meaning of the patient's communications through the resonance of her own internal responses, so the artist listens to the communications of the developing artwork through their effect on her. The artist needs an internal frame that allows her to feel sufficiently safe to be in touch with her inner experience so that she can interact with the developing artwork to find a form that will 'fit'. The artist's training and experience and her resulting confidence in herself as an artist provide the background for the artist's internal frame. Within this frame, reality operates in a different way. Parsons writes about the internal analytic setting:

The internal analytic setting is a psychic arena in which reality is defined by such concepts as symbolism, fantasy, transference and unconscious meaning. These operate throughout the mind, of course. The point about the analyst's internal setting is that, within it, they are what constitute reality.

(ibid.: 1444)

Similarly, within the artist's internal frame, symbolism, fantasy and unconscious meaning constitute 'reality'. Clearly, there is a marked difference between work that takes place within the internal analytic setting and that within the artist's internal frame, in that the analyst responds to the communications of the patient, another subject, whilst the artist responds to the developing artwork, a work that is partly the product of her own internal world. But I am putting forward the idea that the necessary internal frameworks have in common that they provide safe settings within which the analyst or artist can be sensitive to messages from within themselves, and they are both made possible through extended periods of training and experience. In addition to providing herself with a suitable physical space within which she can work with her medium, the artist has to find a space for the developing artwork *in her mind*.

Moving into this 'internal frame' does not happen automatically. It requires a particular effort on the part of the artist to shift away from the concerns of everyday life and into another realm. As Dryden Goodwin puts it:

> *You're constantly trying to be at that point of maximum engagement . . . it's like the idea of breathing underwater . . . of course you can't do that but you submerge yourself and somehow . . . there's a point of anxiety and then 'oh no, I can, I can do it' and I'm in different state but there's a sort of trauma involved in terms of crossing over.*

(Goodwin 2011)

By invoking the risk of drowning, Goodwin conveys a sense of the radical change involved in crossing over into the internal frame. It is like moving from air to water. He gives a sense of what it could feel like to shift into the internal frame but find himself unable to enter a different state of mind. The crossing over is risky and potentially traumatic. It must be followed by the discovery that he can function in this new environment, that he can breathe there after all. He needs to enter a different state of mind, and there is a moment of anxiety before he does so.

The decision to move from one realm to the other is taken with some trepidation. There is a risk involved, and this risk has multiple aspects. Being in the internal artistic frame allows the artist to enter a state of mind in which the boundaries that normally separate the self from the outside world (specifically, the developing artwork) can be relaxed. This in itself may feel dangerous. In addition, the subject of the work may hold its own terrors. These may be overt, as in the case of my own series of works related to Morecambe Bay. It was partly the dangers of the Bay that attracted my interest and evoked the desire to make the work. These dangers in the outside world resonated with internal fears, and my process necessarily involved an engagement with those fears as embodied in the developing artwork. Referring back to the discussion of Parson's paper above, my engagement with aspects of my inner experience as they became embodied in the artwork parallel the analyst's engagement with her inner responses to the patient's material. The analyst needs her 'internal analytic setting' to be in place, and the artist needs her 'internal frame' in order to enter into this engagement.

Given the risks involved, it is not surprising to find that some artists have particular strategies to help them with the difficulty of crossing over. An artist friend tells me that she has to run into her studio and begin work straight away before she has time to prevaricate. One of the interviewees says:

> *I have a set of things that I have to do before I start work if I'm in a studio. When I had my studio in Newcastle, whenever I went in there I would sweep it. I would start every day and I would sweep it even though it didn't need sweeping. But I would do that and that would take about 20 minutes. That would be a way of cleansing my head and clearing away any extraneous stuff, though it was quite unconscious – I didn't know that was what was doing but I would do it religiously every day and then I would start my work.*
>
> *(Bonnell 2011)*

Interestingly, the artist says that she was initially unaware of the essential function of her sweeping. It was done 'religiously', implying a parallel with religious rituals such as repetitive prayer which can be used to induce a meditative state of mind in the participant. The ritual of sweeping becomes an intermediate stage that begins to induce a particular state of mind in the artist. Through the sweeping ritual, she can clear her mind of everyday concerns in preparation for entering her internal frame. The activity has clearly defined time boundaries so the artist knows that this is how long it will take for her to move into her internal frame and her working state of mind. One might speculate that the time limit helps the artist to feel contained and sufficiently safe to embark on the ritual. It will not go on forever. She will not remain caught in an in-between state.

For some artists, particularly painters, an intermediate preparatory stage forms part of their process, as one of the interviewees, Henrietta Simson, describes:

> *For some reason I don't make it easy for myself . . . I'll start from scratch with the board . . . and then mixing pigments into paint as opposed to just painting out of a tube of paint. I don't know why I do that but I do, it's quite a laborious thing . . . maybe that is important . . . maybe there's a lot of thinking that happens actually during that time: not necessarily concerted thinking but more . . . your mind is in a bit of freewheel maybe. As you are kind of painting on your layers of gesso and*

letting them dry, and then painting another layer, and then letting that dry or grinding paint . . . thoughts will come and go, things wash in and out . . . Maybe the physical labour allows my mind to sort of get into a free-wheely type of state or . . . sort of dislocated somehow, just kind of drifting.

(Simson 2011)

Again, Simson indicates that she has adopted particular laborious procedures but she has not previously considered her reasons for doing so. It seems that it is only during the course of the interview that she questions herself about this and discovers a purpose in it. The lengthy physical process of preparing paint and painting surface is a familiar routine that she can follow without focused thought. In this respect, it parallels the sweeping ritual described above. Also, like the sweeping, it occupies a predictable length of time and so opens up a time-boundaried space within which the artist's state of mind gradually shifts from the focus necessary for everyday life to a 'drifting' or meditative state. It seems that, for her, this unfocused state is the necessary prelude to the movement into the internal frame and her working state of mind.

Indeed, although they may not engage in the ritualistic procedures described above, all artists are likely to go through a period of preparation for work as they gather the materials or equipment that they will need. Dryden Goodwin describes his preparation for a photo shoot:

I'm kind of scoping out in the preparation as well as what cameras I'm going to be using, what's the most appropriate lenses to be using for the things I'm interested in capturing. But it's also in terms of a sort of state that I will need to be in to be alert to the things that are, that seem, most potential in that situation and then to be able to be reacted to. . . . it seems to me that a lot of work goes into designing and preparing the circumstances . . . to enable you to be completely involved, to be completely . . . submerged and to be, to lose consciousness within that . . . very particular experience.

(Goodwin 2011)

As Goodwin makes decisions about his choice of equipment, he is setting the scene for his entry into a different state of mind that he describes as a 'submergence' or a loss of consciousness. Here, I understand him to mean a loss of everyday consciousness, although this submerged state of mind includes the ability to be alert to what is going on in the outside world. If his inner frame is safely in place, he will be able to be in tune both with the outside world and with his inner world in order to make decisions about which images to capture. Therefore, it is worth putting 'a lot of work' into 'designing and preparing the circumstances' to set the external frame in place and enable him to enter his internal frame.

This shift from an everyday state of mind to the internal frame can also be thought of as a move into the realm of whatever medium the artist has chosen.

Christopher Bollas, considering the creative person at work with their medium, writes:

> When the painter paints, or the musician composes, or the writer writes, they transfer psychic reality to another realm. They transubstantiate that reality, the object no longer simply expressing self, but re-forming it. This might be considered a type of projection – a putting of the self into an object – but it is also a transubstantial change, where psychic reality leaves its home in the mind and moves into a different intelligence.
>
> *(Bollas 1999: 173)*

I want to consider Bollas' use of the term 'transubstantial object' because I think that he draws attention to an important aspect of the artist's experience and I want to take his ideas a little further. Bollas introduces the term 'transubstantial object' to refer to 'the form into which one moves one's sensibility in order to create: into musical thinking, prose thinking, painting thinking' (ibid.: 176). The idea that the artist moves into a different form of thinking according to the specifics of her medium seems to fit the descriptions of the interviewees. When an artist picks up her paintbrush, she enters a form of 'painting thinking'; when Goodwin picks up his camera, he enters a form of 'photography thinking'. Bollas goes on to assert that 'the "object" through which we create – painting, prose, music – has its own processional integrity, its own laws, and when we enter it to express our idea within its terms, we shall be altered by the object' (ibid.: 176). Here, Bollas emphasises the otherness of the transubstantial object, and this seems to relate to my discussion of the interaction between artist and medium in Chapter 4. He also claims that the artist is transformed by whichever process he chooses. The sculptor Anthony Cragg's statement supports this:

> What I have learned is truly a result of the working of the material. When one works with it long enough, spends time with it and searches, it becomes possible to read ideas and emotions from it . . . Quite literally the sculptor learns from the materials. It is a dialogue with the material . . . When I cause the material to change, I also realise how much it changes me.
>
> *(Goertz 2016)*

Cragg works on his sculptural materials and those materials work on him in their own particular way, a way that differs from one material to another. The result is a new artwork that is not only an expression of the artist's inner experience but a transformation of it, according to the nature of the medium and the form of thinking that medium demands.

Bollas' use of the term 'transubstantial object', together with his suggestion that 'psychic reality leaves its home in the mind', introduces a spatial metaphor in which something from the artist's inner world moves outside into the 'other' territory of the medium's 'language'. But it seems to me that a movement into a different way of *thinking* is an internal process. Nothing has yet become manifest in the outside world. I think that the concept of the transubstantial object conflates two separate aspects of the artist's process – a movement into a *way of thinking* that is peculiar to the medium chosen and the *making* of a new artwork. The movement into a different way of thinking entails a shift to another space *within* the mind, the space that I am calling the artist's internal frame. It is in the *making* of the work that 'psychic reality leaves its home in the mind' and becomes manifest in the developing artwork. Bollas argues for the separateness or outsideness of the transubstantial object through a comparison with the child's introduction to language. He equates the artist's entering into and being transformed by the transubstantial object with the child's entering into and being transformed by language:

> This challenge is not without precedent as at least once we have been presented with the challenge of language, whether to enter it and be transformed by it or whether to refuse speech . . . Art forms offer further challenges to the self and as with language, what emerges from one seems not to be of one's own making, but guided by the form of another.
>
> *(Bollas 1999: 174)*

But I question Bollas' comparison with the child's first introduction to language. For the experienced artist, 'painting thinking' or 'sculpture thinking' is not a new and unfamiliar territory as language is for the young child. Through her training and experience, the artist already knows the characteristics and behaviour of her medium, she has internalised this way of thinking, and it has become an integral part of her 'internal frame'. A painter says that the act of picking up the paintbrush activates all her history of painting. This is *her* history of painting, not painting as a realm separate from her. Dryden Goodwin collects together his photographic equipment and activates his experience as a photographer. The internal frame takes the form of an internal painting frame for the painter or an internal photography frame for Goodwin. Once the artist, held by her internal frame, begins to work with the medium and rediscover its otherness *then* the artist is transformed by her interaction with the medium and the developing artwork reflects this.

Whilst writing this book, I have become acutely aware of the fact that I cannot switch easily from writing to my art practice. The two modes of working, not surprisingly, call for different forms of thinking, but what seems remarkable to me is that the required switch in orientation is so profound that I seem to have to leave one mode of functioning completely before I can begin to prepare myself to engage in the other. Writing a book of this nature is not an artistic endeavour, but this experience does remind me of a period when I was attempting to create an art installation that included photographic images and my own poetry. At that time, I found that I could not work on the visual elements of the work and the poems in tandem. I had to come out of one mode, or one internal frame, and prepare myself to enter the other, and this required both time and mental effort.

Bollas acknowledges the difficulty of moving from everyday life into the new form of thinking:

> An artist does not go easily into this altered state of unconsciousness. They feel the boundary between ordinary psychic life and the artistic workspace, as one that is always difficult to cross and sometimes unbearably so. Even as they become accustomed to entering this other realm they are acutely aware of leaving themselves behind, thrown into a different form of life.
>
> *(Bollas 1999: 173)*

Interestingly, Bollas refers to an altered state of *un*consciousness, implying that this shift involves plunging into the unconscious and, as Dryden Goodwin puts it, a trust that one can 'breathe underwater'. Bollas' emphasis on the unconscious draws attention to the fact that the artist's imbuing of the developing artwork with aspects of her own experience takes place largely out of her awareness. However, I question Bollas' assertion that the artist leaves herself behind. On the contrary, the artists I interviewed claimed that they felt most fully themselves when working. As one artist put it: 'If I'm in a really good zone it's right in there it's all about my real innermost me' (Sian Bonnell). That is, while working, the artist is more fully in touch with her significant inner experience than she is at other times. I think that what the artist leaves behind is not herself but, rather, her focused way of being in the world. However, the difficulty of entering the artistic workspace is rooted partly in the *fear* that the loosening of boundaries between herself and the developing artwork might result in the loss of self.

10

OUT INTO THE WORLD

So it's then about bringing it into the world somehow.

Hayley Newman

The American artist Agnes Martin once said of her paintings: 'The happiest moment is when they go out the door. They go out into the world . . . When they go out I don't take any further responsibility' (Martin 1997). These moments were the culmination of a long process during which she was involved in an intimate relationship with her developing painting. First she would sit in her rocking chair and wait for 'inspiration'. Then she would embark on the long and painstaking process of working with her medium, coercing it into a form to correspond with her internal vision. Finally, she would evaluate the result to decide whether it was ready to go out of the door and have a life of its own.

When Martin judged her painting to be ready to go, this did not mean that she saw it as perfect. She says 'You can't make a perfect painting. We can see perfection in our minds but we can't make a perfect painting' (in Simon 1996: 86). Here, Martin is referring to the fact that the concrete realisation of the artist's idea or pre-sense can never capture its full richness and boundlessness. Therefore, the artist must decide when the work is finished and only she can make this judgement.

So how does an artist know when to stop? How does she decide that a work is ready to go to an exhibition or commissioner? Susan Derges emphasises that a finished work must have the ability to move her:

> I begin with an intuition or a sense of an area I want to explore but it's not fully conscious. At the very end, the way in which I evaluate what I've done . . . depends on whether I'm moved and convinced in a quite visceral or intuitive sense. A piece of work might well do the job but if it doesn't

move me I don't use it; if it doesn't speak to me on multiple levels then I'm not really interested in it . . . it has to be more than an intellectual statement. It has to have the potential to be very much alive . . .

(Derges in Read 2017: 119)

Derges speaks here about the movement from her initial partially conscious 'intuition' (her pre-sense) to a form that moves and convinces her because she can recognise something of herself in it. The work has to live and to 'speak' to her in many ways. In this chapter, I think about how the artist judges that this has been achieved.

One of the interviewees describes the way in which he decides that a work is finished:

> *It's at the point where you think I'd best leave this alone. I think it's as simple as that. It has just reached some point of autonomy . . . where it can fend for itself, it doesn't need me to do anything any more. And I think that . . . in some respects I'd be quite happy if I never saw something again . . . if it works.*

(Aiken 2011)

This artist speaks of the finished work as if it has become a living being that is capable of having its own independent life in the outside world. As was the case for Agnes Martin, it seems that there is some relief in the realisation that the piece now 'works' on its own. Another interviewee, a photographer, speaks about the final stage of editing that marks the end of her process for a particular work:

> *I have to actually kind of get out of myself and look at the stuff with a really open mind and be quite ruthless . . . I am just looking. Letting go of my liking or closeness to it. I have to detach myself.*

(Bonnell 2011)

This artist uses a spatial metaphor here, saying that she 'gets out of' *herself*. In Chapter 5, I discussed the relationship between the artist and her medium in terms of a fluid movement between the 'extended self' state and the 'observer self' state, and I argued that, in the 'extended self' mode, the artist feels herself to be at one with the developing artwork. In the artist's working state of mind, although one or other self-state is uppermost at any moment, the other is never totally absent. Bonnell's description of 'getting out of' herself seems to refer to a movement out of the 'extended self' mode, but this is not merely a movement towards the observer self. The shift she describes is more radical. Now she makes a deliberate choice to change her position in relation to the work. I think that this can be understood as a movement out of the continuum between the extended and the observer self-states. In that continuum, she felt herself to be 'in' the work and now she is 'just looking' at it from the outside. That is, she puts herself in the position of a viewer of the work.

This stepping out of the working state of mind to see the artwork from the outside is also described by sculptor George Meyrick. Talking about leaving his studio at the end of a working day, he says:

> *As the lights go out things really do suddenly spring out in different possible ways . . . It's that mental state of mind. It's a different frame of mind. Absolutely . . . I'm stepping back. I'm finished. I'm not in the middle of and involved in. . . . I'm not looking for anything. It becomes apparent rather than I see it. It just sort of is there and I spot it.*
>
> *(Meyrick 2012)*

As he crosses over into his non-working state of mind, out of the continuum between extended and observer self-states, Meyrick sees his work differently, becoming aware of problems that were obscured when he was closely immersed in it. Most artists do relinquish their working state of mind at the end of the day's work, but Meyrick finds himself looking back at his artwork from this other vantage point. It seems that this is a situation that might occur at any point in his process, not just towards the end. He says that he is 'not looking for anything', suggesting that he has not yet deliberately chosen to adopt a more detached position. This will come later, as his work nears completion.

Dryden Goodwin highlights a point that signals the beginning of the final stage of his process:

> *Sometimes it evolves and it becomes about shedding things, and other times it's about re-introducing something else . . . I suppose most often the initial set of relationships that I was interested in I will return to . . . In terms of making a project . . . it's interesting that kind of critical mass at the point where it seems to start to define itself, it seems to have found its own logic, and then you become, you become the kind of guardian to enable that to fulfil itself . . . that's a really exciting moment.*
>
> *(Goodwin 2011)*

Goodwin seems to be able to identify a particular moment in his process when something important changes, as if at this point he can see a clear way forward. He says that this is most likely to happen when he returns to 'the initial set of relationships' that interested him. This 'initial set of relationships' is the foundation of his pre-sense. He has worked on his project over a period of time, but it is at the point when he re-connects with his pre-sense that the developing work seems to come together. At this point, he recognises that the work has taken on something of his own inner life. He continues:

> *. . . and then you have to make sure that the circumstances that seem necessary for you to complete the edit, or for you to present the work . . ., enable the fundamental elements that you perceive as being essential to articulating the core of the idea. Then there's a certain point that you realise that you could go beyond but that there are*

diminishing returns in terms of how an edit might look or how something might be framed or . . . but you have to get to that point . . . otherwise you can't rest.

(ibid.)

Once he has reached the point when the developing artwork has begun to acquire its own life (a life that is also the artist's own), Goodwin has clarified what the 'fundamental elements' essential to his idea are and now he sets about providing the conditions necessary to embody them. These elements are also fundamental to the artist's pre-sense. He 'can't rest' until he is sure that he has articulated his pre-sense as clearly as he can. Once that point has been reached, further adjustments are no longer essential.

In Chapter 5, I discussed my experience of making *The Transience of Wonder* and the way in which I continually returned to my 'pre-sense' to question what it was about my experience on the mountain that had touched me. Like Goodwin, I could not rest until I felt that the artwork I had produced was in sufficiently close harmony with that experience. As I re-examined my pre-sense, I repeatedly questioned whether the particular elements that I had abstracted from that experience were really the most relevant ones. For instance, I initially thought that the indexical nature of the work was important in that each 'slice' of sky referred to a particular moment in time and space. After I had rejected the timeline print described in Chapter 5, I tried separating the 'slices' and arranging them on a wall according to the altitude differences between each shot (see Figure 10.1).

In this configuration, each 'slice' refers to a particular moment in time and a particular altitude. However, this new incarnation still seemed to be missing something essential. I tried to recapture my memory of my pre-sense to question yet again what it was about that experience that had touched me and what might still be lacking in the work. I realised that my experience was reminiscent of childhood memories of being alone and lying in a field looking up at the sky and the passing clouds. This was associated with a sense of freedom but also of containment as the long grass formed a sort of frame for the sky itself. However, this seemed to be a happy memory, and I felt that there was also a darker side to the experience I was trying to embody that was difficult to capture.

Eventually, I had the prints mounted under thick blocks of perspex so that they became solid objects, 'shards' of sky. It was only at this point that I understood that this was not to be a wall-mounted piece but a three-dimensional installation in which the pieces would be in a 'random' arrangement as if the sky had shattered and fallen to the ground (see Figure 10.2).

I realised that I needed to give up my earlier idea with its emphasis on indexicality because it did not embody my pre-sense sufficiently closely. Through the new configuration, I began to have a clearer sense of the experience I was attempting to capture. I understood that it had something to do with a sense of boundlessness, that as I climbed the mountain the sky lost its framing of trees or of the surrounding landscape, and there was a feeling of emerging into infinite

FIGURE 10.1 *The Transience of Wonder.* Work in progress 2

FIGURE 10.2 *The Transience of Wonder.* Work in progress 3

space. At the same time, this experience was fleeting and unstable, liable to collapse. This verbal description can only give a flavour of the total experience of the pre-sense, but it was this realisation that led me to feel that the work was on its way to being finished. Much work remained to be done in terms of decisions about exact print colours, the number of pieces, the surface on which they would be displayed, the title and so on, but at this point, in Goodwin's terms, the work had 'found its own logic' and I had 'become the kind of guardian to enable that to fulfil itself'.

For installation works, the final form of a piece may depend upon the conditions of the space in which the work is shown. In the case of *The Transience of Wonder*, for its first exhibition, I chose to show the pieces scattered on the grey floor of the gallery (see Figure 10.3).

The choice of a title for a work (even if it is 'Untitled' or, as for Martin Creed, a number) can be an important step in finishing the artwork. Susanne Langer differentiates between the 'presentational symbols' of art that are created anew by each artist and the 'discursive symbols' of language where words have relatively fixed meanings. That is, the words of a particular language are free-standing symbols that represent something other than themselves. Their meanings are understood by anyone familiar with that particular language. By combining words, we can describe something (such as an experience) and talk or think about it. Presentational symbols such as artworks do not describe an

FIGURE 10.3 *The Transience of Wonder.* 30 photographic prints mounted under perspex. Slade School of Fine Art, 2017

experience but, rather, show how the experience feels. Drawing on Langer's work, Ken Wright argues that, in child development, there are two phases of attunement between mother and child. First, the mother responds to the infant with her own facial expressions, gestures and non-verbal sounds, offering presentational symbols that reflect the infant's experiences. Wright compares this to the forms created by the artist. Later, the parents offer the child words and phrases (discursive symbols) to describe his experiences. A vivid example of this was related by a friend who was caring for her young grandchild. The child seemed to be sad and the grandmother said 'You are feeling homesick'. The child immediately brightened, adopting the word and using it for herself. Wright describes this process:

> When words are offered in adaptive ways, they will furnish a verbal envelope to the earlier organization in a way that completes the structure and enables the infant to differentiate and name the experience.
>
> *(Wright 2015: 14)*

In Chapter 4, I discussed Wright's suggestion that the artist coerces the medium to provide the presentational forms that she needs to embody an inchoate element of her inner world. Similarly, she can coerce language to provide a title that will also reflect something of the same inchoate element.

The conferring of a title onto the work (the addition of a discursive symbol to the presentational one of the non-verbal form) can refine or expand the overall form, but this is only the case if the title is not merely descriptive. If the title relates to the visual aspect of the work without being limited by it – if it brings its own associations – then it can act as a vital element of the work. For some artists, the title is decided upon early in the process and is an integral part of the work. For other artists, or for some works, the choice is made towards the end of the process. My own practice is to have a descriptive working title that changes as the work develops. As I begin to recognise myself in the developing form, this working title usually begins to feel inadequate or too limiting, and I replace it with something that seems to take my associations in a different direction. For instance, the working title of *Under the Skin* was *Canal Foot Wall*, a combination of the location in which the photographs were taken and the idea that I wanted to create the sense of a wall of sand. It was only when I saw the way in which the surface of the sand (and of the screen) resembled the skin of a human being, that I gave this piece its final name. This name, in turn, relates to the fact that Morecambe Bay does indeed get under my skin in that it both disturbs and fascinates me. Once I had conferred this title upon the work, it seemed to delineate its separate and autonomous identity.

In order to let go of a new artwork and allow it to take its place in the world, the artist must separate from it in a psychological sense. When the work is completed, the artist relinquishes her state of oneness with it. But this separation may not occur immediately. Indeed, many artists need a period of time to live with the work before they are ready to let it go both psychologically and physically. Agnes Martin waited three days before she allowed a work to be taken for exhibition. Other artists may wait considerably longer, or the letting go may be prompted by a particular event. For instance, Simon Faithfull spoke of a meeting with a curator and a discussion about the future of 'the work' as if it no longer had anything to do with him. This felt 'weird', and it took him a moment to accept that this was the appropriate time to let go and allow the work to have a life of its own (personal communication).

The process of separation is not always an easy one. One of the interviewees, Sian Bonnell, uses the metaphor of birth to describe her experience:

> *It's like an umbilical cord. They are my children you know and I have to cut it. I have to cut and you've got to get yourself to a point where you can do that. You know you've got to do it . . . It's part of me till then and then it's not part of me but there is still a raw thing.*
>
> *(Bonnell 2011)*

This vivid description emphasises the artist's intimate connection with the developing artwork. During the making stage, artist and developing work are bound together by cords that she must now sever, suggesting that this separation is a violent one. She says that she has to get herself to the point where she can make this cut, but the question remains of how she does this.

So how does an artist get to the point of making this separation? In this book, I have traced the artist's journey as she responds to and takes in something from the outside world, works on it internally and, through her interaction with her medium, externalises it in the form of a new artwork, now transformed and imbued with her own inner experience. There remains one more stage of this movement between inner and outer worlds. The final stage involves the artist's recognition that the work does indeed provide a form for an aspect of her inner experience. If it does, she is able to *see* this experience in a new light, and this *seeing* is both visual and intuitive. As an interviewee says: 'I think you see things in a photograph because it is removed from you. It's not inside here, it's physically there and that gives you the space and the distance to see something' (Deborah Padfield).

Through the new form, the artist has a deeper understanding of her own experience. This understanding may or may not be fully conscious. In other words, the artist sees and *takes in* something from the artwork, something that she is now able to integrate. Anton Ehrenzweig writes: 'taking back from the work on a conscious level what has been projected into it on an unconscious level is perhaps the most fruitful and painful result of creativity' (Ehrenzweig 1967: 57). Ehrenzweig suggests that the artist initially projects fragmented parts of herself into the developing work. In the course of her process, these fragments are integrated in the developing work, and eventually the artist is able to take them back into herself. Ehrenzweig's assertion that the artist takes something back *consciously* seems to me to imply a greater level of awareness than may be the case. However, I do think that, if she has been successful, the artist recognises something of herself in the finished work. She senses that the new artwork provides a true form for her experience, although she may not be able to articulate this verbally. John Aiken describes his own sense of recognition and the fact that it may not always be welcome: 'You [sometimes] think "This is an absolutely awful thing that I've made . . . But it's kind of interesting."' This recognition, this seeing her experience in an external form, allows the artist to internalise and integrate it.

But this does not explain why this severing of the close connection between artist and work may, for some artists, be so painful. In Chapter 4, I discussed Wright's characterisation of the artist's engagement with her medium as a reworking of an early relationship between infant and mother in which the medium is used by the artist to perform some of the roles of the mirroring or adaptive mother (Wright 2009a). If this is the case, then to let go of a completed artwork is to lose an ongoing dynamic relationship with a mirroring or attuning 'other'. This could leave the artist feeling bereft. A number of interviewees speak of moving from one project to another and avoiding periods in which they have no ongoing work. For instance, Gina Glover says: 'I don't feel alive if I'm not making work.' In terms of Wright's formulation, this sense of aliveness is related to the struggle to coerce the medium into becoming an attuning form. In other words, the artist feels alive as long as she is *in the process* of enlivening her developing artwork and enabling her medium to become attuned to her. One might suppose that when the artwork is finished and has become a form for her experience, it would continue to act as an attuning form for the artist. But it seems that the feeling of aliveness is not engendered by the relationship between artist and finished work, even though the artwork has now been endowed with its own life or 'vital import'. Rather, it arises from the changing, dynamic dialogue between artist and work in progress. The artist acts on the developing work and that work responds by becoming more attuned to her experience, and it is this fluctuating relationship that makes the artist feel more alive.

To take this further, I return to Winnicott's writing on mirroring. If all goes well enough in infancy, the mother is able to respond to her baby so that her facial expressions and gestures provide forms that fit the infant's experience. Looking at his mother, the infant sees a reflection of himself and this repeated and reliable experience is necessary for his 'going on being' (Winnicott 1963a: 97). Without this mirroring from his caregiver, the infant's development is adversely affected:

> Many babies, however, do have to have a long experience of not getting back what they are giving. They look and they do not see themselves. There are consequences. First, their own creative capacity begins to atrophy, and in some way or other they look around for other ways of getting something of themselves back from the environment.
>
> *(Winnicott 1986a: 112)*

For Winnicott, a person's sense of being alive is integrally connected with his or her 'creative capacity'. As adults, we continue to look for mirroring responses, usually from those people close to us. But, for an artist, a primary way of receiving this dynamic feedback is through her artistic practice, in particular through her work with her medium. Once an artwork is finished, there is a need to move on to another.

The sense of loss that some artists experience when a work is finished may have other components too. Once the artwork leaves the artist, it no longer belongs exclusively to her but is gifted to its viewers who, if they respond to it, will do so because it resonates with their own inner worlds. The writer and psychotherapist Rozsika Parker writes: 'Loss of control at the moment of parting with a piece of work is perhaps the most fearful experience of loss engendered by creativity. Once sold, published or exhibited the meaning of the work becomes constituted by the other' (Parker 1998: 771). Parker emphasises the loss of control here when the meaning of the work (that is, its meaning as an independent art object, not its meaning for the artist herself) is taken over by the viewer. The artist cannot control how the work will be received or whether, indeed, it will be capable of standing on its own without her continuing intervention.

This loss of control over the meaning of the work occurs as soon as an audience experiences it, even if the artist herself is still involved in the presentation of the artwork. The performance artist who performs her own work remains personally and physically involved in the exhibition, and the continuing life of the piece may depend on her physical presence (although it might live on without the artist in the form of its documentation). Artists who use mechanical or electronic equipment may feel that they need to keep a watchful eye on the conditions of exhibition. For the artist who uses other performers, there may be anxieties about whether all is going according to plan. For instance, Martin Creed's *Work No. 850* at Tate Britain (Creed 2008) involved runners in the Duveen Gallery. He speaks of the difficulties of letting go of a performance piece at the point of exhibition: 'Then there's the question of whether or not it's been done properly which is a nightmare to me if you're . . . you know, always having to phone the gallery to make sure it's going on' (Caldwell and Creed 2012). This highlights the differences between the experience of exhibiting paintings, photographs or sculptures that do not change in the showing and exhibiting pieces that continue to demand the artist's attention. In a sense, these latter pieces are always in process of creation, although the artist's control of the medium is less complete.

Creed's anxiety about whether his piece is being done properly brings in the question of the artist's concern about the responses of an audience. This tends to come to the fore in the final stage of preparing a new work of art for exhibition. The artist uses herself as viewer to judge the appearance of the work within the exhibition space. The conditions of the space must complement the form of the artwork itself or, indeed, be part of that form. My installation *Bay Mountain* (discussed in Chapter 6) consists of a pile of sand, built into the shape of a mountain range, onto which a text animation is projected. The animation shows a body of blue text interacting in a wavelike motion with another body of ochre text. This work could only be completed in the venue in which it was to be installed. There I could judge its effect on me (and so, indirectly, imagine its possible effect on an audience) and make any necessary changes:

> *I had to try out Bay Mountain in the gallery space to find out how it would work in practice. What was the best position in the gallery room so that the viewer could walk around the piece and see it from all angles? How far above the sand should I hang the projector? The height affected the dimensions of the projection on the floor so I had to adjust the pile of sand to fit. How much sand did I need? Would the projection run continuously without gaps? Was the room dark enough? Did it matter if there were sounds from other works in the space? How would this affect the experience of the viewer?*

In making these decisions, I considered my own experience of the work and judged each possible configuration in terms of whether or not it 'felt right'. This was a continuation of the stage of working with my medium, but now my medium was the gallery conditions such as the size, position and shape of the pile of sand, the position of the projector and the level of light in the room. At the same time, I was aware that the gallery became the containing space for me as viewer, a frame for the work, and I attempted to display my work in such a way that other viewers might enter into a relationship with it, if it resonated with their own inner experience.

Clearly, at the point of preparing for a specific exhibition, the artist must imaginatively put herself in the place of the viewer as I describe above. But I want to question whether a consideration of the audience may also be relevant earlier in the artist's process. I have left this issue until this late point in the book because I want to emphasise the fact that the artist first and foremost makes the work for herself, in the sense that it must reflect something of her own experience. In order for it to satisfy her, for it to 'feel right', she must come to recognise herself in it. But this is not all that the artwork must do. It must also speak to its audience, not in the sense of transmitting a message (although some works may do this), but rather through its resonance with something in each viewer's own (different) experience. Through the process of making a new work, the artist must *both* link it to her own experience *and* detach it sufficiently for it to have a wider relevance.

Langer's writing about art-making and symbolisation is helpful again here. Langer argues that the creation of an 'art symbol' involves a process of abstraction in which the essential elements of the artist's experience are extracted and irrelevant details are excluded (Langer 1953). These details tie the experience down, linking it exclusively to the artist and to a particular situation. Their removal loosens the artwork's roots in everyday experience and results in a relatively free-floating form that can attach itself to experiences other than those of the artist. That is, the artist creates a form that embodies only the essential elements of her experience, without its other particularities, and it can be responded to by anyone whose own inner experience (with its different particularities) relates to these essential elements.

To take this further, I return to my formulation of the artist's state of mind and the concept of the 'extended self' and the 'observer self'. At this point, I want to consider the role of the 'observer self' in greater detail. Earlier, I characterised the 'observer self' as making moment-to-moment decisions about the direction of the work and the use of the medium, but now I want to consider the basis for these decisions. The central criterion is whether or not any changes bring the work closer to a fit with the artist's own experience. But I think that another factor is also at play. The artist's 'observer self' can also consider whether the essential elements of the developing work are sufficiently prominent and whether they are unclouded by irrelevant detail. In other words, the 'observer self' considers, amongst other things, whether the developing form is sufficiently abstracted to be available to an audience or whether it is too abstracted, so as to have lost touch with its links with the artist's particular experience. It is a delicate balance.

Showing a particular work for the first time is likely to be both exciting and anxiety-provoking. Although the artist may have shown work-in-progress to colleagues or collaborators, audience reactions are never predictable. The artist has got to the point where she recognises the new artwork as a truthful reflector of an aspect of herself. That is, the artwork 'works' for her, but will it 'work' for the audience and, if it does, in what ways will it resonate for them? As described above, she has pared her experience down to its indispensible elements so that other viewers can respond to it in their own way. But only when she shows the work to an audience can she discover whether this abstraction has 'worked'. That is, she discovers whether the artwork operates independently of her experience yet retains enough of its emotional flavour. If the abstraction goes too far and formal considerations predominate, the sense of inner connection may be lost and the work might be experienced as sterile. On the other hand, if the work is too closely connected to the artist's personal experience, if the artist has not abstracted this experience sufficiently, then the work can only resonate with those viewers whose inner experiences are very similar to those of the artist.

11
RECURRING THEMES

Perhaps that continual search for something . . . still looking for this elusive or even illusionary thing . . . is what drives us all on.

John Aiken

Individual artworks do not stand alone. They are connected to the artist's previous work and, in their turn, will influence future work. A number of the interviewees spoke of the way in which concerns explored in one artwork recur in later ones. One interviewee says: 'I think a lot of what I do is repeating the same thing done over and over again in different forms . . . In a way repetition is used to push at something to try to move through it' (Kivland 2011). Since the artwork can never fully embody the inchoate aspect of the artist's inner world, something will always be left undone, and this can re-emerge and be taken further in the next work. One of the artists, Nina Rodin, says:

The finished painting mostly just asks for the next painting. There is no rest, there is no sense of that's done, put a line under it . . . There is still something that you haven't quite touched on or you touch on something new that you hadn't noticed before.

(Rodin 2011)

I think that Rodin is talking about two different situations here. In the first, the artist finds that there is something that they 'haven't quite touched on' in a particular finished work. That is, the finished artwork embodies an aspect of the original pre-sense but another aspect remains to be addressed in a new work. The emphasis is on incompleteness but also on a relatively clear way forward. The second situation is one in which the artist finds that the new artwork touches 'something new that you hadn't noticed before'. This could be something only loosely connected to the original pre-sense, something that might send the artist in quite a different direction or that might lie dormant and re-emerge much later.

Rodin speaks above of how a recently completed painting leads to another. But sometimes an artist revisits a work made some time ago and sees it afresh:

> *A piece of work is a live thing that has the ability to regenerate itself with every experience because we are different every time we go to it. Having to look at it again, it made me realise something else – it made me look at it in a different way.*
>
> (Malacart 2011)

Nearly thirty years ago, I was taking black-and-white photographs and experimenting with various darkroom techniques. I had taken a photograph of a solitary, windswept tree, but when I looked at it, it did not seem to capture the feelings I had when I took the shot. So I tried solarising it, a tricky darkroom technique in those days which had very unpredictable results. Eventually, I came up with an image that embodied the starkness and isolation I had responded to in the tree itself (see Figure 11.1):

The memory of this image stayed with me, and recently I hunted for the original negative, wanting to do something more with it. Now I work mainly with

FIGURE 11.1   Solarised photographic print of tree for *Double Bind*

the moving image, and I wanted to bring this seemingly dead tree to life, to have it grow again. Without consciously intending to do so, I found that I had paired the tree with its reflection. It was no longer solitary but growing, in an uncanny way, towards and away from its reflected image. At a different time in my life, the image had acquired new associations, and my use of a different medium (video animation rather than still photography and darkroom techniques) led to a very different artwork (see Figure 11.2).

Although, for professional artists, the usual culmination of the making process is for the new work to go out into an exhibition or to be delivered to the commissioner, some works of art are of such import for artists that they choose to keep them for themselves. When I was asked to write the catalogue essay for the Danish exhibition *Ikke Til Salg* ('Not for Sale') (Townsend 2015) in which the exhibits were works that the artist chose to keep, I contacted the artists to ask them why they had retained these particular works. Several of the artists replied that they wanted to keep a particular work because they felt that it would be (or had already been) both a turning point and a source of further inspiration. As Jes Fomsgaard writes 'This work has elements and ideas that I don't want to forget. There are questions in this work, I still have to explore' (ibid.: 48). He sees this painting as a 'sourdough' for future artworks. Several artists describe their sense of something within the piece that they cannot yet grasp. Marlene Landgreen says: 'It is the start of something new, some yet unrevealed and not yet, at all, fully explored potential. . . . It is my source, where I find this exact energy, motivation and volume that I want to track more of' (ibid.: 48). The emphasis here is not on incompleteness but on fullness, a superfluity of life and energy, as if the painting were overflowing with possibilities. However, the way forward

FIGURE 11.2 *Double Bind.* 4K video animation, 2018

is not necessarily clear. As Martin Bigum writes: 'It is like a window pointing towards, I do not know what . . .' (ibid.: 48). The potential is not to continue in a familiar way of working but for something different, and the artist may have to wait until the painting reveals this new direction.

Artworks that take the artist in a new direction have done more than provide a form corresponding to the original pre-sense. They have also touched on further areas of the artist's inner world that do not yet have a form. That is, the artist responds to *the new artwork itself* as something in the outside world that resonates with her inner world and gives rise to the intimation that a new artistic direction can be found.

This sense that there is more to be done is essential for the artist's continued urge to create new works:

> *The big worry is when you think 'gosh I've never resolved this properly', or 'I only resolved it at a few different stages', but actually do I want to resolve it? You know, is it something which is just irritating but . . . it will never be resolved? Or if it was resolved is that it? You know, is that it, over? Shutter closed, wrap it up and go home. And I think that perhaps that continual search for something or continual looking at something, and changing perspectives on it but still looking for this elusive or even illusionary thing . . . is what drives us all on.*
>
> *(Aiken 2011)*

There is a paradoxical need to find the perfect form and not to find it. Aiken wants to continue his search and feels that he would be lost without it. This may be partly connected with the sense of aliveness the artist gains through the attuning function of the medium while her work is in progress, as I discussed in Chapter 10. But also, if the 'elusive or even illusionary thing' is the inchoate element of the artist's inner world, then it will necessarily remain elusive since the artwork can never fully encompass it, and it is this very elusiveness that will inspire future works. Each work returns to it, perhaps through a different aspect of the outside world, shedding a different light on it.

Aiken's questioning of himself about whether or not he wants to resolve whatever issue is at the heart of his work brings to mind Winnicott's proposed explanation for the fact that artists never come to the end of their work:

> In the artist of all kinds I think one can detect an inherent dilemma, which belongs to the co-existence of two trends, the urgent need to communicate and the still more urgent need not to be found. This might account for the fact that we cannot conceive of an artist's coming to the end of the task that occupies his whole nature.
>
> *(Winnicott 1963a: 185)*

I think that Winnicott is drawing attention to an important point here. The artwork is intended to communicate the artist's personal experience of some aspect of the outside world, but there is a potential danger. Winnicott's statement above is tied in with his concept of the 'incommunicado self'. He writes: 'I am putting forward and stressing the idea of the *permanent isolation of the individual* and at the core of the individual there is no communication with the not-me world either way. Here quietude is linked with stillness' (ibid.: 189–190). This isolation, according to Winnicott, is healthy and necessary to protect the core self from invasion. If this is so, then the artist must, as Winnicott writes above, strive both to communicate and to keep hidden. But he goes on to suggest that the artist's need not to be found (by the viewer) is the reason why the task of art-making is never-ending. Rather, I think the reason for this lies in the artist's never-ending attempt to *find herself* in her work. This search can never be completed because no artwork can fully capture the inner experience that lies behind the pre-sense. There is always something left out.

In Chapter 10, I related the artist's continuing need to find herself to Wright's notion of the developing artwork as a mirror (in the Winnicottian sense) and suggested that the completed artwork is no longer in a dynamic relationship with the artist, and therefore cannot continue to perform this mirroring function for her. In order to re-engage in a mirroring process, she must turn to a new work. These ways of thinking about the artist's need to continue to create new works are related to Winnicott's view of creativity as necessary in everyday living and as rooted in early experiences. To feel alive, we need to create the outside world for ourselves by imbuing it with our own inner experience. That is, we do not, in health, respond to elements of the outside world as if they are fixed in meaning and essentially dead. Rather, we search (not necessarily consciously) for elements that resonate with us on a personal level. This is the basis of the artist's pre-sense, but it also occurs in everyday activities for artists and non-artists alike. A reader of a novel picks out a particular passage that seems to speak to her, a cook alters a recipe to make it her own, a gardener arranges her garden in a particular way. In everyday ways, we continually strive to see the world afresh. When we do so, we not only recreate an element of the outside world but we also renew ourselves. That is, we break down and recreate *ourselves* by taking in and integrating the new experience. In this way, we are always in the process of self-realisation, a process of destruction and creation that is never completed. To continue this process, we must continue to 'live creatively'. For the artist, this is achieved not by completing a new work but by being engaged in the process of creating. When one work is finished, another must be started.

The interviewees give their own reasons for their need to continue creating art. For some, each work calls for another because 'The work is never as good as you think it's going to be' (Edward Allington). For others, one artwork may spark many new associations that can be pursued in different ways:

> So, a piece of work I made ten years ago, I am still articulating it. I'm still talking about it and reframing it in terms of current work that I'm doing. It just keeps on, keeps on going and has many layers to it.
>
> (Newman 2011)

Another interviewee also speaks of a linkage between different works:

> *I think what's really important for me is a sense of a continuum in the practice, in my practice, and that in the different contexts and locations that I've looked at they share certain qualities, certain frequencies of . . . of engagements between people but also certain emotional nuances as well. But also that in this idea of the continuum that there are shifts as well.*

(Goodwin 2011)

Goodwin's 'continuum' relates to ongoing themes that are manifest across works related to many different elements of the outside world. In a variety of situations, Goodwin is looking for certain qualities in common. It seems likely that these qualities relate to something of personal importance to him and that he experiences a pressure to find forms to embody this 'something'.

I want to highlight two different ways in which ongoing concerns may recur in different works. In the long-term search described by Aiken and Newman, they speak of deep personal themes that recur in separate works relating to different aspects of the outside world. On the other hand, an artist may make a series of works, all related to a single outside element. I will illustrate the difference between these two situations through a consideration of my own work.

Taking the example of my series of works related to Morecambe Bay, this began with the sense that there was something about the Bay that both fascinated me and made me uneasy. This led, through a series of stages, to the first idea for a new work. The resulting artwork *On the Shores*, a montage of still and moving images reflecting on the hazardous journey across the Bay, shed some light on the aspect of my inner world that had been activated by the Bay (see Figure 11.3).

FIGURE 11.3 *On the Shores.* SD video, 2009

It also offered me a new vision of the Bay and, correspondingly, a different way of relating to it.

Having completed the first work, I felt that there was more for me to explore. *On the Shores* had emphasised the Bay as an expanse of water, and I wanted to make another work that would focus more closely on the quicksands. This resulted in another video piece, *The Quick and the Dead* (discussed in Chapter 3) that shed a different light on my inner experience of the Bay. The series continued in this way with several more works, all related to the Bay, each new form elaborating further on my experience of this particular landscape.

After exhibiting *Under the Skin* (see Figure 8.1), one of the series of works related to Morecambe Bay, I noticed for the first time that the portrait format of the projection and its dimensions resembled previous works in different media and related to different elements of the outside world. In 2000, I had created an installation of 12 steel panels inscribed with text (see Figure 11.4) and the shape and size of each panel was similar to that of *Under the Skin*.

In 2007, I created another installation, *Witches' Dance* (see Figure 11.5), comprising photographic prints on silk, and, again, each silk panel resembled the projection in terms of its dimensions.

I was aware that, in both those earlier works, I consciously intended the format to relate to the dimensions of a female figure. This led me to recognise that, outside my conscious awareness, the same desire was present in the new work and that I was, in this piece as in the previous ones, exploring my relationship with an internal maternal image. Reflecting on these pieces in relation to each other also led to the realisation that, across the three works, there was a movement towards

FIGURE 11.4 *Ecclesia Mater.* 12 inscribed steel panels, photographs. Globe Gallery, Hay-on-Wye, 2000

FIGURE 11.5 *Witches' Dance.* 8 photographic prints on silk. Dock Museum, Barrow-in-Furness, 2007

increasing animation of the 'figure'. In the earliest piece, the steel panels were rigid and unmoving. In the second, the photographs on the silk panels were of solid rock, but this immutability was belied by the flexibility of the silk and its tendency to move in the breeze created as visitors moved through the gallery. For the latest piece, I animated still photographs to create a constant movement as if the sands themselves were alive. It seems that presentations, more or less disguised, of a maternal image are an ongoing theme in my work and the motif appears in artworks that arise from very different aspects of the outside world.

At this point, I want to consider how the recurrence of personal themes might be thought about in terms of psychoanalytic theory. I have said that the artist is driven to find a form for an inchoate element of her inner experience, but this leaves open the question of the nature of this inchoate element. Freud saw art as providing disguised forms for repressed material, presenting this material to the artist herself and to others in a veiled way. He also developed the concept of repetition compulsion whereby a person may repeat or re-enact a repressed traumatic experience again and again. So is the artist who repeatedly returns to the same theme caught up in a repetition compulsion? The repetition compulsion serves to avoid rather than to elaborate; there is no forward movement. But in this book, I argue that the making of art can promote self-development. Bollas sheds some light on this complex issue. He introduces the concept of 'genera' (see also Chapter 2), contrasting it with trauma and using the term to refer to the ability to select elements and aspects of the outside world that will promote self-development. The person takes these elements into the receptive unconscious (as opposed to the repressed unconscious) for 'incubation' or gestation (Bollas 1992b). This may, for an artist, lead to a new work of art, as I have described earlier in the book. In Bollas' terms, this is a process of 'symbolic elaboration'. But, according to Bollas, 'the effect of trauma is to sponsor symbolic repetition, not symbolic elaboration', and this route could also lead to new artworks. He continues: 'Nonetheless, certain writers, painters, musicians, and so forth only ever repeat themselves, and their works are valued as significant symbolizations of human life – which they no doubt are' (Bollas 1992b: 69–70). In this book, I have been concerned only with the route of 'symbolic elaboration', but this is not to deny the fact that artworks can also be created from a position of trauma and repression.

Repression implies that what is to be repressed has already been given some sort of form before it is denied access to consciousness. The psychoanalyst Howard Levine re-examines Freud's definition of the repressed (Freud 1915) and points out that:

> The distinction that Freud was making was between the organized, articulatable subset of the unconscious that we call the repressed or dynamic unconscious and the second, more extensive category of inchoate forces that either lost or never attained psychic representation and, although motivationally active, were not fixed in meaning, symbolically embodied, attached to associational chains, etc.
>
> *(Levine 2012: 607)*

These 'inchoate forces' may have their roots in infancy when the infant was dependent on his caregivers to provide forms for his experience through mirroring (Winnicott 1986a) or attunement (Stern 1985), but even the most sensitive mother will not offer perfect forms for every experience. Indeed, it is likely that the infant's states of rage and distress would present particular difficulties in this regard. Inevitably, then, each person has a vast residue of experiences that have never been given form and cannot be brought to consciousness. Levine argues that there is an internal pressure to find forms for these states, and he calls this pressure the 'representational imperative'.

Here, I am concerned with the ways in which the practice of art may provide a route towards finding forms for aspects of these 'inchoate forces'. These states are not accessible to consciousness and can never be fully apprehended. Certainly, they cannot be pinned down by the fixed representational symbols of verbal language. But the more open, presentational forms of art are ambiguous and multiply determined. At a conscious level, the artist may be aware of working on a particular issue but, outside her awareness, other factors may operate. Taking the example of my realisation that different bodies of work all assume the shape of a female form, when I was in the process of creating the last work, *Under the Skin*, I was unaware of this repetition. It seems that, outside my awareness, there was a 'representational imperative' to return to this theme. I am suggesting that these themes relate to inchoate states in me, but that they do not, and can never, completely capture those states. Rather, each artwork relating to a particular theme *points towards* something inchoate and sheds light on some aspect of it. Some artists deliberately and consciously return to certain themes during their working lives. But here I put forward the proposition that, whether they are aware of it or not, themes are likely to recur in an artist's work, and these themes may relate to aspects of inchoate states that are pushing to be given form. Moreover, since the inchoate can never be apprehended in its entirety, there will always be a need to continue making work in an attempt to approach it ever more closely.

POSTSCRIPT

When I began the research that underpins this book, I wanted to focus on the question of *how* artists make work and to skirt the thorny issue of *why* they do so. I had experienced for myself that the making of art is a life-enhancing activity, but I wanted to avoid a reductionist approach in which art is seen primarily as a form of self-therapy. The diverse concerns of artists in their work extend far beyond their personal inner issues. But already I am making a distinction between inner and outer, and herein lies the issue that is at the heart of this book. The artist, like anyone else, is affected by those aspects of the outer world that touch her personally. That is, her experience of the outer world is affected by the inner so that the distinction between the two cannot easily be maintained. For this reason, I have turned to the writing of D.W. Winnicott, whose theory of transitional phenomena acknowledges and explores the intermediate space between inner and outer worlds. The overlap of the inner and outer is also relevant to the parallel questions of *how* and *why* the artist makes work. In the course of conducting this research, I have found that the two questions are inextricably linked with each other and that it is not possible to address the *how* without touching on the *why*. However, I have addressed the question of *why* only in a very general way, making no attempt to consider the personal motivations of individual artists.

On a number of occasions, creative people working with other artforms have told me that ideas I put forward in this book have struck chords for them, and they have asked whether the findings of my research are also relevant to poets, musicians and creative writers. Does a poet have a 'pre-sense' before starting a poem? Does a composer enter an 'internal frame' when starting work? An adequate answer to these questions would call for another study (or two), but it does seem likely that many of the findings might also apply to the other arts. I suspect that there are both parallels and differences. Thinking about parallels, it may be that creative persons in other artforms also experience a 'pre-sense' heralding a new work, that they too need an 'internal frame' and enter a particular state of mind (the 'extended self') while working. For example, composer Philip Glass comments that: 'when you're writing you're so focused on what you're doing. You don't see yourself writing. The activity requires all of our attention . . . The "we" that can comment on it is not there during the act of creating' (in Midgette 2018). This sounds very like the state of mind I have called the extended self. Writer Rose Tremain begins her novels with what she calls 'the first mystery', an image that comes to mind as if from nowhere (Boylan 1993). This image is not yet an idea for a new book, but it has an emotional resonance and sets Tremain on a path of exploration much as the pre-sense does for the artist. For the poet Richard Hugo, a new poem is often triggered by his response to an unfamiliar town, but he knows that it is not the town itself that is the 'real' subject of his poem. That 'real' subject, one that is of personal significance, will only emerge later through his working with the words of the poem and their sounds (Hugo 2010). Hugo's 'triggering subject' parallels the element of the outside world that leads to the artist's pre-sense, whilst his interaction with the words of the emerging poem parallels the artist's relationship with her medium. The novelist John Fowles writes of: 'the acute pleasures of the writing of "pre-natal" or pre-separation stage, with the published book equalling full awareness of separate identity' and goes on: 'my being centres in the processus . . . and its delights and has only a very peripheral attachment to the "born" (also "dead") book' (in Rose 1987: 161). This relates closely to the interviewees' experience of completing and separating from their work and of their need to be always in the process of creating. When the artwork or book is 'born', to use Fowles' language, it gains its own separate life but, paradoxically, it may seem 'dead' to its creator as she is no longer in a living dialogue with it.

One of the differences between the experiences of creative writers and visual artists (or musicians) is that the medium of creative writing is language and language is also the medium of rational thought. The visual artist is (usually) dealing with a non-verbal medium and can, perhaps, more easily lose herself in the work (in the 'extended self' mode) whilst the poet or creative writer may need to give herself strategies to avoid a takeover by the 'observer self'. Richard Hugo advises his poetry students to focus initially on the sounds of the words rather than their meaning. Writer V.S. Pritchett says that he does not start by thinking up a plot but by selecting a character based on someone he has encountered. The character leads the evolving story in ways that its author did not foresee (Boylan 1993). The poet Jacob Polley sees ideas as dangerous for a poem. If he begins to write with an idea in mind, he feels he is finding something that he has 'already thought' and the freshness of the poem may be lost. He tells his students: 'Don't start with an idea. Start with a phrase, start with some kind of music, start with something that's interesting that you've seen or touched or felt and then explore' (Polley 2015). In the terms introduced in this book, Polley seems to be encouraging his students to be alert for a pre-sense. But he does not want them to take the pre-sense forward into an idea before starting work on a poem. Rather, the poem must evolve through the writing. This is a similar method to that adopted by those painters who start to make marks on their canvas without a specific idea and who allow the work to evolve through their interaction with the medium.

Artists are a very diverse group of individuals, each of whom has his or her own particular story to tell. In working towards a coherent narrative, I have been obliged to leave out many fascinating details of individual experience that would have deflected the reader from the central trajectory of the book. Although the artist quotations give some sense of the wealth of detail in the interviews, this book can do no more than give a flavour of their full richness. However, many of the artists have generously given their permission for the audio recordings to be held in the British Library where they will be available to all. Details of how to access them can be found in the Appendix.

This book describes the artist's process in terms of an interplay between inner and outer worlds and depicts the artist as concerned not only with her own self-realisation but also with objects and issues in the world of shared reality. At its heart is the argument that the artwork *both* provides a form for a previously unformed inner experience *and* presents some aspect of the outside world in a new way. This is the essence of the 'newness' of the artwork. It lies in the uniqueness of this particular artist's response to this particular element of the outside world and the form that is given to the experience by this particular use of a medium. In imbuing the developing artwork with something of her own inner life, the artist also vivifies the outside 'something' that is the subject of the work, presenting it in a new and vital way. The artwork becomes a space in which inner and outer worlds coincide, first for the artist and then for the viewer.

APPENDIX

Archiving of interviews

Of the 33 interviews recorded for the qualitative research study, agreement was obtained for 25 to be archived at the British Library Sound Archive as part of the Oral History collection.

The British Library's oral history collection is one of the most extensive in the world and includes interviews in a vast range of subjects, including many collections relating to the arts. For more information on oral history at the British Library, see www.bl.uk/oralhistory or contact oralhistory@bl.uk.

All the interviews have summaries and several have verbatim transcripts. The interviewees who agreed to deposit their interviews at the British Library assigned their copyright in the recordings to the British Library. Patricia Townsend has retained her copyrights until April 2033, after which rights are transferred to the British Library. All the recordings are catalogued on the British Library Sound and Moving Image catalogue (http://sami.bl.uk) and can be accessed at the British Library, subject to any access restrictions requested by individual interviewees. The collection title is *Interviews exploring artists and the creative process* and the collection reference is C1801. The references for individual artists are:

John Aiken interviewed by Patricia Townsend (reference C1801/02).
Edward Allington interviewed by Patricia Townsend (reference C1801/01).
Sian Bonnell interviewed by Patricia Townsend (reference C1801/03).
Alfonso Borragan interviewed by Patricia Townsend (reference C1801/04).
Susan Collins interviewed by Patricia Townsend (reference C1801/05).
Chris Drury interviewed by Patricia Townsend (reference C1801/06).
Simon Faithfull interviewed by Patricia Townsend (reference C1801/07).
Gina Glover interviewed by Patricia Townsend (reference C1801/08).
Dryden Goodwin interviewed by Patricia Townsend (reference C1801/09).

David Johnson interviewed by Patricia Townsend (reference C1801/10).

Sharon Kivland interviewed by Patricia Townsend (reference C1801/11).

Laura Malacart interviewed by Patricia Townsend (reference C1801/12).

George Meyrick interviewed by Patricia Townsend (reference C1801/13).

Russell Mills interviewed by Patricia Townsend (reference C1801/14).

Eleanor Morgan interviewed by Patricia Townsend (reference C1801/15).

Hayley Newman interviewed by Patricia Townsend (reference C1801/16).

Hughie O'Donoghue interviewed by Patricia Townsend (reference C1801/17).

Deborah Padfield interviewed by Patricia Townsend (reference C1801/18).

Sarah Pickering interviewed by Patricia Townsend (reference C1801/19).

Liz Rideal interviewed by Patricia Townsend (reference C1801/20).

Henrietta Simson interviewed by Patricia Townsend (reference C1801/21).

Kay Tabernacle interviewed by Patricia Townsend (reference C1801/22).

Estelle Thompson interviewed by Patricia Townsend (reference C1801/25).

Jon Thomson and Alison Craighead interviewed by Patricia Townsend (reference C1801/23).

Jo Volley interviewed by Patricia Townsend (reference C1801/24).

BIBLIOGRAPHY

Abella, A. 2007. Marcel Duchamp: on the fruitful use of narcissism and destructiveness in contemporary art. *International Journal of Psycho-Analysis*, 88, 1039–1059.

Abella, A. 2010. Contemporary art and Hanna Segal's thinking on aesthetics. *International Journal of Psycho-Analysis*, 91, 163–181.

Abella, A. 2013. Psychoanalysis and art: from applied analysis to interdisciplinary dialogue. *Art in Psychoanalysis*. London: Karnac and the International Psychoanalytical Association.

Abts, T. 2013. Interview with Simon Grant in *Where Is Painting Now*. *Art Quarterly*, Winter 2013, 58.

Aiken, J. 2011. John Aiken interviewed by Patricia Townsend (reference C1801/02). *Interviews exploring artists and the creative process*. London: The British Library.

Allington, E. 2011. Edward Allington interviewed by Patricia Townsend (reference C1801/01). *Interviews exploring artists and the creative process*. London: The British Library.

Amirsadeghi, H., & Homayoun Eisler, M. 2012. *Sanctuary: British Artists and Their Studios*. London: Thames and Hudson.

Barlow, P. 2012. Conversation with Frances Morris. *Through the Writings of Louise Bourgeois: New Perspectives on Art and Psychoanalysis*. London: Courtauld Institute of Art.

Bickers, P., & Wilson, A. (eds.) 2007. *Talking Art: Interviews with Artists since 1976*. London: Art Monthly and Ridinghouse.

Blumenthal, K. 1974. Interview with Agnes Martin. *On Art and Artists*. Chicago: School of the Art Institute of Chicago, Video Data Bank.

Bollas, C. 1992a. The evocative object. In *Being a Character: Psychoanalysis and Self Experience*. London and New York: Routledge.

Bollas, C. 1992b. Psychic Genera. In *Being a Character: Psychoanalysis and Self Experience*. London and New York: Routledge.

Bollas, C. 1992c. Aspects of Self Experiencing. In *Being a Character: Psychoanalysis and Self Experience*. London and New York: Routledge.

Bollas, C. 1999. Creativity and psychoanalysis. In *The Mystery of Things*. London and New York: Routledge.

Bollas, C. 2018. The spirit of the object as the hand of fate. In *The Shadow of the Object: Psychoanalysis of the Unthought Known*. Abingdon: Routledge.

Bonnell, S. 2011. Sian Bonnell interviewed by Patricia Townsend (reference C1801/03). *Interviews exploring artists and the creative process*. London: The British Library.

Bourgeois, L. 2012. *Psychoanalytic Writings*. London: Violette Editions.

Boylan, C. (ed.) 1993. *The Agony and the Ego: The Art and Strategy of Fiction Writing Explored*. Harmondsworth: Penguin.

Caldwell, L., & Creed, M. 2012. *Making Space*. Conference at University College London, 25 February.

Caper, R. 1996. Play, experimentation and creativity. *The International Journal of Psycho-Analysis*, 77, 859–869.

Collins, S. 2014. Susan Collins interviewed by Patricia Townsend (reference C1801/05). *Interviews exploring artists and the creative process*. London: The British Library.

Creed, M. 2000. Work No. 232. The whole world + the work = the whole world. London: Tate Modern.

Creed, M. 2008. Work No. 850. London: Tate Britain.

Csíkszentmiháyi, M. 1996. *Creativity*. London: Harper Collins.

Ehrenzweig, A. 1948. Unconscious form-creation in art. *British Journal of Medical Psychology*, 21, 185–214.

Ehrenzweig, A. 1962. Unconscious mental imagery in art and science. *Nature*, 194, 1008–1012.

Ehrenzweig, A. 1967. *The Hidden Order of Art: A Study in the Psychology of Artistic Imagination*. London: University of California Press.

Eigen, M. 1983. Dual union or undifferentiation? A critique of Marion Milner's view of the sense of psychic creativeness. *International Review of Psycho-Analysis*, 10, 415–428.

Faithfull, S. 2012. Simon Faithfull interviewed by Patricia Townsend (reference C1801/07). *Interviews exploring artists and the creative process*. London: The British Library.

Fortnum, R. (ed.) 2007. *Contemporary British Women Artists*. London and New York: I.B.Tauris.

Freud, S. 1910. Five lectures on psycho-analysis. *The Standard Edition of the Complete Psychological Works of Sigmund Freud*, Volume XI, 1–56.

Freud, S. 1915. The unconscious. *The Standard Edition of the Complete Psychological Works of Sigmund Freud*, Volume XIV, 159–215

Freud, S. 1916–1917. Introductory lectures on psycho-analysis. *The Standard Edition of the Complete Psychological Works of Sigmund Freud, Volumes* XV–XVI.

Freud, S. 1925. Negation. *International Journal of Psycho-Analysis*, 6, 367–371.

Freud, S. 1937. Constructions in analysis. *The Standard Edition of the Complete Works of Sigmund Freud*, Volume XXIII, 255–270.

Glover, G. 2011. Gina Glover interviewed by Patricia Townsend (reference C1801/08). *Interviews exploring artists and the creative process*. London: The British Library.

Goddard, J. 2011. Judith Goddard interviewed by Patricia Townsend.

Goertz, R. 2016. Anthony Cragg: parts of the world. Video recording. Bonn: Institut für Kunstdokunmentation.

Goodwin, D. 2011. Dryden Goodwin interviewed by Patricia Townsend (reference C1801/09). *Interviews exploring artists and the creative process*. London: The British Library.

Hugo, R. 2010. *The Triggering Town: Lectures and Essays on Poetry and Writing*. New York and London: W.W. Norton.

Johnson, D. 2011. David Johnson interviewed by Patricia Townsend (reference C1801/10). *Interviews exploring artists and the creative process*. London: The British Library.

Jones, W., & Perry, G. 2007. *Grayson Perry: Portrait of the Artist as a Young Girl*. London: Vintage.

Kivland, S. 2011. Sharon Kivland interviewed by Patricia Townsend (reference C1801/11). *Interviews exploring artists and the creative process*. London: The British Library.

Klein, M. 1929. Infantile anxiety-situations reflected in a work of art and in the creative impulse. *International Journal of Psycho-Analysis*, 10, 436–443.

Klein, M. 1940. Mourning and its relation to manic-depressive states. *International Journal of Psycho-Analysis*, 21, 125–153.

Klein, M. 1946. Notes on some schizoid mechanisms. *International Journal of Psycho-Analysis*, 27, 99–110.

Langer, S.K. 1942. *Philosophy in a New Key*. Cambridge, MA: Harvard University Press.

Langer, S.K. 1953. *Feeling and Form*. New York: Scribner.

Langer, S.K. 1957. *Problems of Art: Ten Philosophical Lectures*. New York: Scribner.

Levine, H.B. 2012. The colourless canvas: representation, therapeutic action and the creation of mind. *International Journal of Psycho-Analysis*, 93, 607–629.

Lovett, L. 2011. Leah Lovett interviewed by Patricia Townsend.

Malacart, L. 2011. Laura Malacart interviewed by Patricia Townsend (reference C1801/12). *Interviews exploring artists and the creative process*. London: The British Library.

Martin, A. 1997. Interview with Agnes Martin by Chuck Smith and Sono Kuwayama, online. Available: http://vimeo.com/7127385.

Matte Blanco, I. 1980. *The Unconscious as Infinite Sets: An Essay in Bi-Logic*. Abingdon: Routledge.

McDougall, J. 1995. Sexuality and the creative process. *The Many Faces of Eros*. London: Free Associations.

Meyrick, G. 2012. George Meyrick interviewed by Patricia Townsend (reference C1801/13). *Interviews exploring artists and the creative process*. London: The British Library.

Midgette, A. 2018. 81 and going strong, Philip Glass prepares for his Kennedy Center debut. *The Washington Post*, 7 March.

Mills, R. 2011. Russell Mills interviewed by Patricia Townsend (reference C1801/14). *Interviews exploring artists and the creative process*. London: The British Library.

Milner, M. 1952a. The role of illusion in symbol formation. In *The Suppressed Madness of Sane Men*. London: Routledge, 1987.

Milner, M. 1952b. The framed gap. In *The Suppressed Madness of Sane Men*. London: Routledge, 1987.

Milner, M. 1957. *On Not Being Able to Paint* (2nd edn.). London: Heinemann.

Milner, M. 1967. The hidden order of art. In *The Suppressed Madness of Sane Men*. London: Routledge, 1987.

Milner, M. 1987. *The Suppressed Madness of Sane Men: Forty-Four Years of Exploring Psycho-analysis*. London: Routledge.

Mitchell, J. 2012. The sublime jealousy of Louise Bourgeois. *The Return of the Repressed*, ed. P. Larratt-Smith. London: Violette.

Morgan, E. 2011. Eleanor Morgan interviewed by Patricia Townsend (reference C1801/15). *Interviews exploring artists and the creative process*. London: The British Library.

Newman, H. 2011. Hayley Newman interviewed by Patricia Townsend (reference C1801/16). *Interviews exploring artists and the creative process*. London: The British Library.

O'Donoghue, H. 2013. Hughie O'Donoghue interviewed by Patricia Townsend (reference C1801/17). *Interviews exploring artists and the creative process*. London: The British Library.

Padfield, D. 2011. Deborah Padfield interviewed by Patricia Townsend (reference C1801/18). *Interviews exploring artists and the creative process*. London: The British Library.

Parker, C. 1988–1989. *Thirty Pieces of Silver.* London: Tate.

Parker, C. 1991. *Cold Dark Matter: An Exploded View.* London: Chisenhale.

Parker, R. 1998. Killing the angel in the house: creativity, femininity and aggression. *International Journal of Psycho-Analysis,* 79, 757–774.

Parsons, M. 1999. The logic of play in psychoanalysis. *International Journal of Psycho-Analysis,* 80, 871–884.

Parsons, M. 2000. Creativity, psychoanalytic and artistic. *The Dove that Returns, The Dove that Vanishes.* London and Philadelphia: The New Library of Psychoanalysis and Routledge.

Parsons, M. 2007. Raiding the inarticulate: the internal analytic setting and listening beyond countertransference. *International Journal of Psycho-Analysis,* 88, 1441–1445.

Peppiat, M. 2012. *Interviews with Artists, 1966–2012.* New Haven and London: Yale University Press.

Podro, M. 2007. Destructiveness and play: Klein, Winnicott, Milner. In *Winnicott and the Psychoanalytic Tradition: Interpretation and Other Psychoanalytic Issues,* ed. L. Caldwell. London: Karnac.

Polyani, M. 1962. *Personal Knowledge: Towards a Post-Critical Philosophy.* London: Routledge and Kegan Paul.

Polley, J. 2015. Jacob Polley, interview. Lyric, University of Sheffield, NowThenMag.

Qureshi, I. 2016. *Where the Shadows Are So Deep.* London: Barbican Curve.

Rayner, E. 1981. Infinite experiences, affects and the characteristics of the unconscious. *International Journal of Psycho-Analysis,* 62, 403–412.

Read, S., & Simmons, M. (eds.) 2017. *Photographers and Research: The Role of Research in Contemporary Photographic Practice.* New York and London: Routledge.

Rideal, L. 2011. Liz Rideal interviewed by Patricia Townsend (reference C1801/20). *Interviews exploring artists and the creative process.* London: The British Library.

Robinson, K. 2017. Creativity in everyday life (or living in the world creatively). Conference paper, Newcastle, 25 November. [A version of this paper is published in *Donald W. Winnicott and the History of the Present: Understanding the Man and His Work.* London: Karnac, 2018, 77–89.]

Rose, G. 1987. *Trauma and Mastery in Life and Art.* New Haven: Yale University Press.

Roussillon, R. 2010. The deconstruction of primary narcissism. *International Journal of Psycho-Analysis,* 91, 821–837.

Roussillon, R. 2015a. Creativity: a new paradigm for Freudian psychoanalysis. In *Playing and Reality Revisited: A New Look at Winnicott's Classic Work,* ed. G. Saragno and C. Seulin. London: Karnac.

Rousillon, R. 2015b. An introduction to the work on primary symbolization. *International Journal of Psycho-Analysis,* 96, 583–594.

Sabbadini, A. 2013. In between and across. In *Art in Psychoanalysis: A Contemporary Approach to Creativity and Analytic Practice,* ed. G. Goldstein. London: Karnac and the International Psychoanalytical Association.

Sandler, J. 1976. Countertransference and role-responsiveness. *International Review of Psycho-Analysis,* 3, 43–47.

Schutz, D. 2013. Interview with Charlotte Mullins in *Where Is Painting Now?. Art Quarterly,* Winter, 59.

Segal, H. 1952. A psycho-analytical approach to aesthetics. *International Journal of Psycho-Analysis,* 33, 196–207.

Segal, H. 1957. Notes on symbol formation. *International Journal of Psycho-Analysis,* 38, 391–397.

Segal, H. 1974. Delusion and artistic creativity: some reflexions on reading 'The Spire' by William Golding. *International Review of Psycho-Analysis*, 1, 135–141.

Segal, H. 1978. On symbolism. *International Journal of Psycho-Analysis*, 59, 315–319.

Segal, H. 1991. *Dream, Phantasy and Art*. London and New York: Routledge.

Simon, J. 1996. Perfection is in the mind: an interview with Agnes Martin. In *Art in America*, 84, 82–89.

Simson, H. 2011. Henrietta Simson interviewed by Patricia Townsend (reference C1801/21). *Interviews exploring artists and the creative process*. London: The British Library.

Stern, D. 1985. *The Interpersonal World of the Infant*. New York: Basic Books.

Stiles, K., & Selz, P. 2012. *Theories and Documents of Contemporary Art*. Berkeley, Los Angeles, and London: University of California Press.

Stokes, A. 1934. The stones of Rimini. *The Critical Writing of Adrian Stokes, Vol.1 (1930–1937)*. London: Thames and Hudson.

Stokes, A. 1937. Colour and form. *The Critical Writing of Adrian Stokes, Vol.2 (1937–1958)*. London: Thames and Hudson.

Stokes, A. 2014. *Art and Analysis: An Adrian Stokes Reader*. London: Karnac.

Thompson, E. 2017. Estelle Thompson interviewed by Patricia Townsend (reference C1801/25). *Interviews exploring artists and the creative process*. London: The British Library.

Thomson, J., & Craighead, A. 2011. Jon Thomson and Alison Craighead interviewed by Patricia Townsend (reference C1801/23). *Interviews exploring artists and the creative process*. London: The British Library.

Townsend, P. 2013. Making space. In *Little Madnesses: Winnicott, Transitional Phenomena and Cultural Experience*, ed. Annette Kuhn. London: I.B. Tauris.

Townsend, P. (ed.) 2014. Psychoanalysis and artistic process. *Free Associations*, 65.

Townsend, P. 2015. Art and the inner world. Catalogue essay, *Ikke Til Salg Trapholt*. Karen Grøn. Denmark: Narayana Press.

Townsend, P. 2017. Between inner and outer worlds. In *Photographers and Research: The Role of Research in Contemporary Photographic Practice*, ed. S. Read and M. Simmons. London: Routledge.

Turner, J.F. 2002. A brief history of illusion: Milner, Winnicott and Rycroft. *International Journal of Psycho-Analysis*, 83, 1063–1082.

Volley, J. 2011. Jo Volley interviewed by Patricia Townsend (reference C1801/24). *Interviews exploring artists and the creative process*. London: The British Library.

Wallas, G. 1926. *The Art of Thought*. London: Jonathan Cape.

Winnicott, C., Shepherd R., & Davis, M. 1989. *Psychoanalytic Explorations: D.W. Winnicott*. London: Karnac.

Winnicott, D.W. 1942. Why children play. *The Child and the Outside World: Studies in Developing Relationships*. London: Tavistock.

Winnicott, D.W. 1953. Transitional objects and transitional phenomena: a study of the first not-me possession. *Playing and Reality*. Harmondsworth: Pelican, 1986.

Winnicott, D.W. 1956. Primary maternal preoccupation. *Through Paediatrics to Psycho-Analysis*. London: Hogarth, 1975, 300–305.

Winnicott, D.W. 1958. Psycho-analysis and the sense of guilt. *The Maturational Processes and the Facilitating Environment: Studies in the Theory of Emotional Development*. London: Hogarth Press and the Institute of Psycho-Analysis, 1965.

Winnicott, D.W. 1963a. Communicating and not communicating leading to a study of certain opposites. *The Maturational Processes and the Facilitating Environment: Studies in the Theory of Emotional Development*. London: Hogarth Press and the Institute of Psycho-Analysis, 1965.

Winnicott, D.W. 1963b. The development of the capacity for concern. *The Maturational Processes and the Facilitating Environment: Studies in the Theory of Emotional Development.* London: Hogarth Press and the Institute of Psycho-Analysis, 1965.

Winnicott, D.W. 1963c. From dependence towards independence in the development of the individual. *The Maturational Processes and the Facilitating Environment: Studies in the Theory of Emotional Development.* London: Hogarth Press and the Institute of Psycho-Analysis, 1965.

Winnicott, D.W. 1968. Playing: its theoretical status in the clinical situation. *The International Journal of Psycho-Analysis,* 49, 591–599.

Winnicott, D.W. 1986a. Mirror-role of mother and family in child development. *Playing and Reality.* Harmondsworth: Penguin.

Winnicott, D.W. 1986b. Playing: a theoretical statement. *Playing and Reality.* Harmondsworth: Pelican.

Winnicott, D.W. 1990. *Home Is Where We Start From.* Harmondsworth: Penguin.

Wright, K. 1991. *Vision and Separation.* Northvale, NJ, and London: Jason Aronson.

Wright, K. 2009a. Found objects and mirroring forms. T-PACE workshop, Slade School of Fine Art, 21 November.

Wright, K. 2009b. *Mirroring and Attunement: Self-Realization in Psychoanalysis and Art.* London and New York: Routledge.

Wright, K. 2014. Maternal form in artistic creation. Conference paper, *Dialogues between Psychoanalysis and Art.* Newcastle, 22 November.

Wright, K. 2015. The circus animals' desertion. *Rivista di Psicoanalisi,* LXI (4), 1–21.

INDEX

References to illustrations are in **bold**